GAME OF MY LIFE

PENN STATE

NITTANY LIONS

GAME OF MY LIFE

PENN STATE

NITTANY LIONS

MEMORABLE STORIES OF NITTANY LIONS FOOTBALL

JORDAN HYMAN
FOREWORD BY MICHAEL ROBINSON

SPORTS
PUBLISHING

Sports Publishing books may be purchased in bulk at special discounts for sales promotion, corporate gifts, fund-raising, or educational purposes. Special editions can also be created to specifications. For details, contact the Special Sales Department, Sports Publishing, 307 West 36th Street, 11th Floor, New York, NY 10018 or sportspubbooks@skyhorsepublishing.com.

Sports Publishing® is a registered trademark of Skyhorse Publishing, Inc.®, a Delaware corporation.

Visit our website at www.sportspubbooks.com

10 9 8 7 6 5 4 3 2 1

Library of Congress Cataloging-in-Publication Data is available on file.

ISBN: 978-1-61321-071-0

Printed in the United States of America

To my wife, Jeannine, for her loving support, firm
encouragement, and passionate enthusiasm.
Sorry for hogging the computer.

And to the countless denizens of Nittany Lion Nation—your
loyalty will always inspire me.

CONTENTS

A NOTE FROM THE AUTHOR

The day Joe Paterno died, long after my kids were asleep, I flipped on the lights in the basement and began sorting through file folders and several stacks of gunmetal gray Maxell C90 cassette tapes. I knew it was in there. And I knew what was on it. I just felt like listening for awhile.

I slipped the tape labeled "JOE PATERNO" into our family's circa 1985 D-battery-powered dinosaur of a cassette player, the kind used to blasting Peter Pan and Mary Poppins soundtracks as Julia, Jackson and Justine fade into Never Never Land. Tonight it played Joe Paterno's Brooklyn-born bark.

Sandi Segursky, Paterno's longtime executive admin, had arranged this particular interview. Turned out to be less difficult than I thought it would be. I explained everything to her by phone, how I was writing a booked called *Penn State Game of My Life*, focused on pivotal games and popular moments in Penn State's rich football history.

My approach to the project was haphazard at best, and it seemed to work. Go for the biggest names, and if and when that failed, go for the more easily attained interview subject to speak to the must-have triumphs from the last sixty years or so of Nittany Lion lineage. There are 19 such "Games of My Life" in this reprinted edition of the original. The book initially had 20 chapters. The one that's missing was about the guy whose actions ultimately cost Paterno his job and, some might argue, his life. (I should note that I am not, and never will be, in that camp. Joe did not die of a broken heart. The cancer got him first.)

Sandi set up the call. Paterno agreed to speak for thirty minutes. And he was right on time—no surprise there.

We made some brief chit-chat. He asked me if I was related to Merv Hyman, the longtime *Sports Illustrated* writer and editor, who had teamed with *New York Times* sports reporter Gordon White to write *Football My Way*, which was published in 1971. I am not a relative of Merv's, but this was not the first time I'd been asked.

Paterno recalled that Merv Hyman had a daughter who once attended Penn State. "I didn't know whether you were a grandson," said Paterno that night in March 2005, his voice full and his words far more clear than in many press conferences of the last few years. "If you're as good as Merv was, you're pretty good."

I stumbled around looking for a segue to jump into my prepared list of questions for "Game of My Life." Joe interrupted my rambling compliments of Merv.

"What are you doing anyway?" he asked. "Sounds like a screwy idea. But go ahead."

I paused the tape and laughed out loud to myself. It was vintage Joe. A twenty-seven-year-old former Collegian reporter lands a book deal with, gulp, a small cash advance, then spends the better part of six months calling, researching, interviewing, transcribing, writing—rinse, wash, repeat. He gets to the curtain, earns thirty minutes with Oz himself, and "Sounds like a screwy idea" is the icebreaker Coach uses to open the phone interview.

In hindsight—a popular word these days in State College—Joe's witty summation made sense. Say what you will about Paterno's actions or inactions in the Sandusky dealings of the last decade plus. Defend him, or don't. Doesn't matter to me.

The fact is, Paterno used every chance he had to tell anyone who would listen things like, "We try to remember, football is part of life—not life itself."

Yet, ironically, his life *was* football. Rather, all the good he gave the world was made possible through football.

Paterno saw himself as a teacher. That's fairly well documented. It's why in 1973 he turned down $1.3 million over five years to become head coach of the New England Patriots, a job he initially accepted, then changed his mind upon realizing he was "flattered by the dough." As Rick Reilly once wrote, that salary package was about $1.25 million more than PSU was paying Joe in those days.

As Paterno's wavy grays whitened in the 1990s and the questions about retirement amplified, he often said pacifying things about wanting to leave "meat on the bone" for his successor. Then he would shift to talking about his health, and how, if he was healthy, he'd like to coach "a couple more years." Two, three, five, 10. Time just steamed along.

My guess is Paterno likely never intended to leave anything for anyone. He just wanted to coach and teach. Succession plans be damned.

"I'm alive," he said to a roomful of reporters in 2005. "I don't want to die. Football keeps me alive."

Football gave Joe entree to the lives of students, parents, and erstwhile sportswriters. It let him be that educator he saw himself as. It allowed him to be part coach, part comedian, part wise guy, part tough guy, part parent, part grandparent. It wasn't necessarily about "game of my life" so much as it was just about life. The games and memories preserved in this book were only important to Paterno because of the people behind the stories and all the people behind all the other great Penn State football stories that aren't in here.

He gave thousands of people a chance to have the game of their life, simply by having lived long enough to influence them.

$$* \ * \ *$$

I could see the seconds counter on my phone, and I knew time was running short. When Sandi says, "Joe will give you thirty minutes," she means, "Joe will give you thirty minutes."

At about the twenty-eight-minute mark, long after Joe had given me most of his recollections on his first game as a head coach—a 1966 win against Maryland, after which Terps coach Lou Saban skipped the traditional postgame coaches handshake, later telling Paterno by phone that he ran off the field because he was so embarrassed about how poorly both squads had played—I was out of questions. Beyond bottom of the barrel. Flat out of questions.

Fearful that dead air would cause Joe to cut the call short, I started in with, "I know you don't think ahead like this, but if you could paint the perfect ending to the Joe Paterno Era at Penn State, how would you paint it?"

I know. I know. Awful question. Ranks right up there with some of the worst I'd ever heard asked of a PSU coach or football player. Almost as bad as, "LaVar, if you could be any animal in the world, what animal would you be?" (True question. I kid you not.)

"Oh gee," was Paterno's first-blush response to my clichéd query. He paused for what seemed an unnatural amount of time.

"I know I'm putting you on the spot," was all I could muster. Again with the cursed dead air.

"I know," he said. "I haven't even thought of that really. I think you gotta just—I don't care what you do. You're gonna write a story. You might want to write the greatest story that's ever been written or the greatest article that's ever been written. You gotta take care of the details. You gotta dot the i's and relook at the sentences and restructure the paragraphs.

"It's the same way with my business. I gotta just pay attention to the little things and try to make us as good as we can be. We have guys in the right spot; are we asking them to do things they can do? Is there something they can do better so we would be more productive? It's an ongoing evaluation of all the little things to combine to make the big things."

I thought he was finished. This was starting to sound familiar. Then Joe went for the close.

"You know, you back away from a story two weeks after you've written it and say, 'Dammit, why didn't I do this?' And for others you say, 'Jeez, that was pretty damn good.' It's the same story. If I ask you where you want to be thirty years from now, you hope you'll still be able to sit down and write a good story."

I stopped the tape again. I let the last line reverberate in the silence of the basement. Then I pressed play once more.

I heard myself trying to sneak in a follow-up by asking about recruiting. But the counter on the phone had hit thirty minutes.

"I don't mean to be rude, but I gotta..." Joe said, his famously nasal pitch trailing off, this time for effect.

I thanked him for his time and offered to e-mail him a draft of his *Game of My Life* chapter to Sandi Segursky for him to check out before it went to press. I knew it would have to go through Sandi; Joe wasn't big on e-mail.

"Good deal," he said. "Good luck. When do you think you're gonna get that out?"

"It'll be out before the 2006 football season."

"Good for you. Make sure you reevaluate each sentence. OK?"

"Thanks, Coach."

"OK. Bye-bye now."

The stop button snapped loudly and my Maxell C90 ceased winding.

Joe Paterno was gone. And I knew when our tears dried, we'd all be OK, regardless of which games we chose to play in our lives.

All we'd ever have to do is listen.

—Jordan Hyman, April 2012

FOREWORD
By Michael Robinson

C hoosing the "game of my life" isn't easy. In the 2005 college football season alone, I experienced more unforgettable moments in a Penn State uniform than I can count on my throwing hand: Rallying on the road to beat Northwestern on my fourth-quarter touchdown pass to Derrick Williams; beating Ohio State at home under the lights; sealing the Big Ten title in the regular season finale; outlasting Florida State in triple overtime in the Orange Bowl. The list goes on.

Even if pressed to pick a single top game, I'd have to pass. Rather, I'd elect to tab the entire journey of the 2005 campaign as a collective game of my life. Because in my eyes, retelling the story of just one contest from that magical season would be incomplete without acknowledging the other 11.

I'm sure the 20 players featured in Jordan Hyman's *Penn State: Game of My Life* faced similar dilemmas. But in reading through the book's chapters, it became clear not only why each former Nittany Lion selected the game he did, but also why Penn State football will always hold a special place in my heart. Because the details captured in this text—the rivalries, the upsets, the friendships, the coaches, the bowl games—remind me in many instances of my own memories from my years in the program. The times and circumstances may vary, but the themes of hard work, dedication, vindication, and brotherhood still resonate with me.

Whatever I go on to do in the NFL, I know I'll always be part of something special called Penn State football. It's a unique history that I'm honored to have played a part in, a history Hyman has deftly accessed in this book. These 20 stories will take you back in time into the lives of some of your favorite players from years past. So enjoy the ride. I know I sure did.

We Are! Penn State!

INTRODUCTION
By Jordan Hyman

J oe Nastasi had one question. "You sure you want me?" he asked, after I'd explained the *Game of My Life* concept. "Absolutely," I told him, launching into my reasons why the former Penn State wide receiver should be the subject of one of my 20 chapters.

Sure, Nastasi's fake field goal-scoring touchdown to beat Michigan in the 1995 Snow Bowl hadn't clinched a Big Ten championship or set some school record. But it *had* set off another flurry of snowballs, wrenched from beneath the icy aluminum benches of the student section in Beaver Stadium's south end zone. And it had remained, well, frozen in Nastasi's mind for the decade since.

That November day was marked by frenzies of flying white pellets that stopped game clock, drew undecipherable tirades from Joe Paterno, and, amid it all, made Nastasi a legend. What's more, it was a moment in time that Penn Staters, whether they were snug on their couches or chiseling snow from their boots in the upper reaches of the Beav, will not soon forget.

Such moments in time sweeten this book and help explain why each former Nittany Lion selected his particular game of my life. They are memories of momentous occasions that changed a man's life. Gregg Garrity's *Sports Illustrated* cover-gracing Sugar Bowl score on New Year's Day, 1983. Craig Fayak's 34-yarder that silenced the Notre Dame echoes in 1990. A fall day in 1966 when Paterno jogged onto the Beaver Stadium grass for the first time as head coach of the Nittany Lions.

They are tales of youth before players like Jerry Sandusky and Lenny Moore became Nittany Lion legends. They are bold performances that have helped the program grow and prosper. John Cappelletti's 41 carries for 220 yards to stave off N.C. State in 1973. Wally Triplett's color barrier-breaking appearance in the 1948 Cotton Bowl. Shane Conlan's eight-tackle, two-interception night in the

Arizona desert to help pull off the upset of upsets in the 1987 national championship game.

They are sentimental, and they are unforgettable. And wrapped as one, the recollections, revelations, and replays of these 20 men—their memories span 53 football seasons—spell out a delectable collection of chapters in the rich history of Penn State football. And I loved writing each of them. Even yours, Joe.

1

WALLY TRIPLETT

NAME: Wallace Triplett III
BORN: April 18, 1926, in La Mott, Pennsylvania
HOMETOWN: La Mott, Pennsylvania
CURRENT RESIDENCE: Detroit, Michigan
OCCUPATION: Retired Chrysler manager; former NFL player
POSITION: Halfback, defensive back
HEIGHT: 5 feet, 10 inches
PLAYING WEIGHT: 165 pounds
YEARS LETTERED: 1946 to 1948
NUMBER WORN AT PSU: 12
ACCOMPLISHMENTS: First African-American to start and earn a varsity letter at Penn State; one of three African-Americans on 1947 Nittany Lion team who broke the Cotton Bowl's color barrier; scored six touchdowns in 1948 season to lead Penn State in scoring; remains second all-time in school history with 16.5-yard average on punt returns; selected by the Detroit Lions in 19th round of the 1949 NFL Draft, then became the first African-American draftee to play in the league; once had 294 return yards in a game for Detroit, an NFL record that stood for 44 years.
THE GAME: The Cotton Bowl, Penn State versus Southern Methodist, January 1, 1948

The Young Life of Wally Triplett

Wally Triplett will tell you that his life's accomplishments are a matter of good timing, and indeed, the successes and travels of his life might leave you with a Forrest Gump-ish vibe. But there's more to his story. Behind Triplett's easygoing banter and unassuming nature is a former football player who still embodies all the greatness of perhaps the finest football team ever to suit up at Penn State.

It all seemed so improbable considering his roots. Wally was the fifth of six sons born to Mahlon and Estella Triplett, who raised him and his brothers in the Philadelphia suburb of La Mott, Pennsylvania. The Triplett kids, all of whom graduated from nearby Cheltenham High, were natural athletes. And each brother imparted different nuggets of sports knowledge on young Wally, who would play basketball, baseball, and football at Cheltenham.

Of all sports, it was football that tied the family together. All six boys played. "I was always hoping to do as well as my brother ahead of me, who was really great," Triplett says of older brother Fred. "And I learned a lot. You were expected to do certain things, and there's no reason you shouldn't."

Triplett's parents, and later his older brothers, worked for the U.S. Postal Service. In high school, Wally worked there too. He made special deliveries, which earned him access to a car or motorcycle plus a Class-A gasoline stamp, two rare perks at a time when the U.S. was imposing a stringent gas ration because of the ongoing World War. "I had a car and gas," he says with a smile, "so that was big with the girls."

Triplett could have started a career with the USPS like the rest of his family, but as the speedy halfback developed on the gridiron, his coaches at Cheltenham High began planning bigger things for him. It helped that Triplett was well above average in the classroom. Though he didn't land a football scholarship after his senior year in 1945, he qualified for a state-funded academic award called a senatorial scholarship, and thus departed for Penn State in the fall of 1945 on a full academic ride. He left La Mott knowing nothing about the university, including its exact whereabouts, carrying just a few

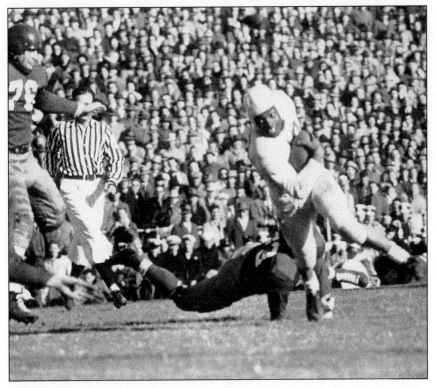

Wally Triplett was one of three African-American players on Penn State's roster to break the Cotton Bowl's color barrier in 1948. He later became the first African-American NFL draft pick to play in the league.

belongings and a letter addressed to Coach Bob Higgins to help land him a roster spot on the football team.

The Setting

In 1945, the same year the U.S. dropped atomic bombs on the Japanese cities of Hiroshima and Nagasaki, Triplett arrived in State College. It didn't take him long to settle in. After initially checking into a hotel, Triplett learned the football staff had arranged for him to live in Lincoln Hall, a boarding house off Atherton Street on the west side of campus. Hurting for spending money, he took a job as a dishwasher in the nearby bus station.

Friends came easily, thanks to his warm, approachable personality. He grew close with his Lincoln Hall roommate, Barney Ewell, who happened to be one of the world's fastest sprinters, a track star who won a gold and two silver medals at the 1948 Olympics. Meanwhile, several members of the football team needed help with their studies, so Triplett would tutor whomever required assistance. He forged bonds with his new, mostly white teammates such as Sam Tamburo and the Drazenovich brothers, Chuck and Joe. Tamburo, a lineman from New Kensington, Pennsylvania, eventually became Triplett's best friend on the team and, later, an All-America end in 1948.

Coach Higgins was another story. The sometimes grumpy coach envisioned Triplett as the second coming of another black player at Penn State in the 1940s, Dave Alston, a superior athlete whom Higgins once called "the greatest player I ever coached, the first player I've seen who has all the qualities that made [Jim] Thorpe the great star he was." But Alston never actually lettered at State—he died suddenly in 1941 following a tonsillectomy. "I was shocked like everyone else when he died," Triplett says. "It was a social thing at the time, where he didn't get the best treatment and ended up dying."

When Higgins first met Triplett that fall of 1945, he told the freshman about Alston. But Triplett knew the stories; he'd idolized Alston growing up, having followed his superb all-county career as a prep star at Midland (Pennsylvania) High School and then on to the Penn State freshman team. "I told [Higgins] I would not be able to replace [Alston]," Triplett says, "'cause I didn't think I could. So he and I hit it off kind of poorly."

Triplett's relationship with "The Hig" hardly improved in the ensuing months. Higgins was never jazzed that Triplett was tutoring his football players, especially if it made them free thinkers, which Triplett clearly was at that time—especially on racial issues. Once, during his high school days, Triplett had been selected to go backstage and meet African-American actor, singer, and civil rights activist Paul Robeson after a speech, and Robeson's ideals of equality resonated with the young man. Triplett refused to accept things as they were.

For example, when one professor continually gave Triplett failing grades on his papers, he enlisted the help of a white woman in the community whom he'd befriended along with a doctor of psychology who lived in Lincoln Hall. They decided to have the doctor secretly write one of Triplett's papers, and Triplett would submit it as his own. When that too came back with a poor mark, Triplett and his friends took the evidence to college administrators, and Penn State decided not to renew the bigoted professor's contract. The incident, of course, didn't warm Higgins' opinion of Triplett.

"The Hig was something else," Triplett says of his coach. "He and I never hit it off, and we went through school like that, because I was always asking questions of why. Sometimes I didn't understand his thinking. He would just say, 'Awwww, ya know, Wallace …

"Hig wasn't a bigot, but he was typical of most white people at the time. They wanted things to be better, but they weren't willing to give up some of what they had to see that things were made equal."

Penn State posted a 6-2 record in 1946. Triplett wouldn't have seen much time that year if not for the departure of Joe Tepsic, who played one season for Higgins in '45, then signed a baseball contract with the Brooklyn Dodgers. (In '47, when the Dodgers came to Philadelphia's Shibe Park, Triplett sometimes went to visit Tepsic, which is how Triplett first met Jackie Robinson. Trip and Robinson later played in the same pinochle gang and shared the occasional meal of hot rolls and greens at a place called Mom's in Philadelphia.)

With Tepsic gone, Triplett had the chance to display his speed on offense, while also satisfying his jones for banging heads on defense. "We used to love to stuff 'em," he says of he and his defensive mates. "We would get mad with each other out there. I remember Chuck Drazenovich was mad as hell if you let somebody get in that hole for 3 or 4 yards. So we'd be arguing with each other the whole time we were out there. But that's what helped us.

"I remember one game, the officials were laughing about it. 'Man, for you guys to be playing with each other, you're not friends!' They were laughing that they were having to break up fights among us."

In Triplett's era, there were two groups: the older players, guys in their mid-20s like Larry Joe, Joe Colone, and Dennie Hoggard (another African-American player who had played briefly in State College before joining the Army to fight in World War II); and the non-veterans, teenaged freshmen like Triplett. Higgins felt a closer bond to the older players who had left and come back from war. And while that veteran core helped the 1947 team earn its famous "Men of '47" nickname, the magic of that season could not have happened without the youthful exuberance of its young players.

The age gaps rarely impacted unity off the field. In '47 Penn State was to play Miami in Florida, the stipulation being that the Nittany Lions' black players could not suit up. Higgins wanted to go, but he opted to let the players decide. "That's when the shock of my life came," Triplett says. "Some of the guys like Neg Norton and John Potsklan said, 'Look, we play together, we stay together.' The coaches were told we wouldn't go to Miami."

Wherever Penn State did go in '47, it dominated. Bucknell, 54-0. Fordham, 75-0. Navy, 20-7. Pittsburgh, 29-0. By Thanksgiving, the Lions had completed a 9-0 regular season with six shutouts to win the first of 22 Lambert trophies in school history. The defense allowed 3.8 points a game that season, a school record, and 17 yards rushing per contest, the lowest average in NCAA history. That unit also still holds the NCAA mark for fewest total yards allowed in a single game (minus-47 in a 40-0 blanking of Syracuse). On the flip side, with guys like Triplett, Elwood Petchel, and Fran Rogel in the backfield, the offense chewed up 2,713 total rushing yards, another school record that stood for 21 years.

Still, with only four bowls at the time, there were no givens. Only when Southern Methodist agreed to play Penn State with its black athletes did the Nittany Lions seal a bowl berth. It was billed as the best of the East versus the best of the Southwest, led by SMU's "Mr. Everything," All-American Doak Walker. And it lived up to the hype.

The Game of My Life
By Wally Triplett

THE COTTON BOWL
PENN STATE VERSUS SOUTHERN METHODIST
JANUARY 1, 1948

I remember we took a train to get to Dallas for the Cotton Bowl, which took two days. When we got down there they gave us these 10-gallon hats and took pictures of us. The only place we could stay was the Navy base outside town. None of the hotels would take us because of Dennie and myself and Charlie Murray. That's something we never got used to, but we said, "We'll take it out on the field."

In the days before the game, there were a number of things going on in Dallas in the colored section. A guy from the *Pittsburgh Courier*, the largest Negro newspaper at that time, squired us around. For example, two top high schools were having their big game at the Cotton Bowl, and they had a pregame beauty contest. I was one of the honorary judges.

One night some of the Penn State alumni down there who had done well arranged for the team to come and visit this big bank they were showing off. We were on our way back to the Navy base that night when we went past this big nightclub on the highway. The driver was explaining that this was one of the featured nightclubs of the area. All the older guys were yelling, "Let's go to the club!"

So we pulled in. We had two buses. As we stopped, I said to Red (team manager David Barron), "Oh man, I don't know if we can go in here." So Red told everybody to hold up. He goes to the doorman and explains we were the Penn State football team and wanted to see the show. The doorman goes in and gets the owner, and the owner says, "Yeah, we want you in." Then he grabs me by the elbow and says, "We ain't never had no niggers in here, but you come on!"

By that time they'd scraped up some tables and seats and people were very cooperative. Girls were throwing their legs up and stuff. I said, "Man, you gotta be crazy!" I ordered a Coca-Cola and my eyes were in the bottom of the glass. I wasn't looking at that stuff. But it was a fun thing.

We had heard so much back then about this Doak Walker. When the game started, they scored right away and we said, "Oh man, looks like it's gonna be a hard day." But we made the adjustments. I remember I kept saying to Petchel, "I can get out in that corner." I eventually convinced him, Petchel threw the thing out there, and I caught it for a touchdown. I was telling him we could have done this all day.

We should have won that game easy. For one, we missed the extra point. Ed Czekaj's extra point would have won the game for us. It was close. I never saw it because I was out there blocking. Later on the tapes, it looked like we missed it. We also had a chance to win at the end, and there was a pass over the middle to Dennie, but somehow it was deflected and dropped.

I saw the ball on the ground, so I knew that was it. I turned and headed right for the locker room. I had a test coming up and had to get back to school, so I had booked a flight to get me out of there right after the game was over. But when I headed for the locker room, I didn't know Doak Walker was coming to congratulate me or shake my hand or say hi. It looked like I just walked away from him. I didn't know until I had gone home and was reading about it, and they said I had snubbed Doak Walker. When I saw him later, I explained it.

As for the game, it ended the way it started. When you have two teams that are unbeaten and they go out with a tie, that's as good as it can get.

Game Results

No. 4 Penn State had indeed heard a lot about Doak Walker before the 1948 Cotton Bowl, just Penn State's second bowl ever. And by the looks of things early on that New Year's Day, it seemed the Nittany Lions believed the hype. In windy, near-freezing conditions, Walker, who would win the Heisman in '48, and the No. 3 Mustangs racked up nearly 200 yards of first-half offense, with Walker throwing for one score and passing for another. A "home" crowd—of the 43,000 fans in house that day, only 3,000 had received tickets from Penn State—was ecstatic. The only hiccup came when Walker, hurried by a charging John Wolosky, missed an extra point.

Down 13-0, Penn State changed the momentum late in the first half when Petchel hit Larry Cooney for a 38-yard scoring strike. Triplett saved a touchdown just before halftime by shoving Paul Page out of bounds on a kickoff return.

In the third quarter, Penn State tied it on Petchel's 6-yard toss to Triplett. Then came Czekaj's fateful point-after attempt. His boot sailed high above the uprights, and the officials' hesitancy added to the drama. Finally, the kick was ruled wide right, though there were some who for years afterward maintained the kick was good.

Both teams had opportunities to take leads later in the game, but the defenses were stout. State held SMU to 24 yards passing and 15 rushing in the second half. The Mustangs, meanwhile, intercepted Petchel twice in the second half, recovered a fumble, and stopped State on downs in SMU territory.

On the game's final drive, Penn State moved the ball to SMU's 37 and called timeout with two seconds left. The Lions then tried 48-Sweep Pass, and Hoggard broke open in the end zone, but a Mustangs defender deflected the ball and it hit Hoggard in the stomach, bouncing harmlessly to the ground. Wrote Jere Hayes of the *Dallas Times Herald*, "It was one of the most thrilling Cotton Bowl games ever unreeled."

Reflecting on State

After a 1948 senior season in which Triplett led the Nittany Lions in scoring and all-purpose yardage—'48 was also Higgins' last season as State's coach, as he retired for health reasons—the speedster became the first African-American NFL draft pick to play in the league. But

Triplett doesn't consider himself a trendsetter for that, especially considering how many black players had signed pro contracts and were already excelling in the upstart All-America Football Conference at the time. It was all timing. Plus, had Branch Rickey offered more cash, Triplett would have signed with Rickey's Brooklyn Dodgers football team. "But he was cheap in baseball and football," Triplett says, "so he and I didn't hit on it. I said, 'The heck with you.'"

The kid from La Mott instead signed with the team that drafted him, the Detroit Lions, for $5,000. At the time, it was more than his father earned in a year working for the Postal Service. It was even more than his longtime acquaintance, Jackie Robinson, had made when Rickey first signed him to baseball's version of the Dodgers.

In his 1949 rookie season, Triplett set a team record for longest run from scrimmage by scampering 80 yards for a score against Green Bay. After his second year in the league, he made history again by becoming the first NFL player drafted into military service for the Korean War. He never saw action, and when he returned from the Army, the Lions traded him to the Chicago Cardinals, for whom he played two seasons before retiring in 1953.

Triplett's done a bit of everything in the half-century since hanging up his cleats. He taught at Philadelphia's Ben Franklin High School. When he returned to Detroit, he worked as a manager at one of Chrysler's stamping plants. He later spent time in the insurance business, worked as a clerk in the horse racing industry, even owned a liquor store. For wife Leonore's birthday in 1973, he bought a motor home, and the couple spent years taking trips across the country. "Each one of our kids was able to put their feet in both oceans and across both borders," he says.

There aren't many of the "Men of '47" alive today. "We're getting to where we'll fit in a phone booth," Triplett jokes. Ask him how he's doing, and he cracks another one: "Answering the bell. Not moving as quick, but answering the bell." If there's anything he talks more seriously about, it's being on a '47 team that stuck together and changed stereotypes about blacks and whites coexisting on the same squad. It all makes sense when he mentions how his Penn State days changed his life.

"I began to look at things a little different," Triplett says. "I began to understand you could find bigotry in some of the highest places, and you could find some of the greatest people in the world in some of the lowest places. You had to search yourself and get in there with them and say, 'Well, this is life. Let's live it and not be afraid.'"

2

ROSEY GRIER

NAME: Roosevelt Grier
BORN: July 14, 1932, in Cuthbert, Georgia
HOMETOWN: Roselle, New Jersey
CURRENT RESIDENCE: Los Angeles, California
OCCUPATION: Program administrator, community affairs for the
    Milken Family Foundation; public speaker; former NFL player
POSITION: Defensive tackle, defensive end, offensive lineman
HEIGHT: 6 feet, 4 inches
PLAYING WEIGHT: 242 pounds
YEARS LETTERED: 1951 to 1954
NUMBER WORN AT PSU: 74
ACCOMPLISHMENTS: Four-year starter at Penn State selected
    by New York Giants in third round of 1955 NFL Draft; played
    11 pro seasons, seven with New York, four with Los Angeles
    as part of Rams' Fearsome Foursome defensive line; received
    Penn State's Distinguished Alumnus Award in 1974;
    humanitarian, musician and author also built performing
    career as an actor in multiple movies and TV shows, including
    Daniel Boone, The Danny Thomas Show, and *Movin' On.*
THE GAME: Penn State at Illinois, September 25, 1954

The Young Life of Rosey Grier

Roosevelt Grier was just a kid living with his parents and 10 brothers and sisters on rented government farmland in Cuthbert, Georgia, when he decided he was going to be different from peers and siblings—different from the stereotypes. To get there, Roosevelt knew he'd have to get an education that would serve as a foundation for his future. Plus he'd have to cover his chores.

"Before I could go to school, I had to achieve the work I would have done had I not been going to school," says Grier of his time in Cuthbert. "And my parents were no schoolaholics. If I went to school, fine. If I didn't, it was still all right. So I had to beg to go to school."

His crowded life comprised three components. First came those chores: He had to slop the family hogs, milk the cows, work in the cotton and peanut fields, and do anything else required of him. Second came school. And third, well, there was walking to and from school, a 20-mile, round-trip hike on foot. It didn't leave time for sports or goofing around or much else.

Grier's lifestyle—he went by Roosevelt, not Rosey, for much of his youth—changed dramatically when he was 11 years old. That year he and his family moved north to live with an aunt who'd purchased a house in Roselle, New Jersey. The Griers sold all their belongings, gave back their government land and cooked enough chicken to last them a three-day, Georgia-to-Jersey train ride. Once in the Garden State, law mandated that Grier go to school, which was fine by him. No more 20 miles of walking on top of daily farm work. "I loved going to school," he says. "I had made up my mind a long time ago that I was not gonna work on a farm or carry a paper bag to lunch every day."

As his parents labored just to scrounge enough income to feed his large family—dad Joseph worked at nearby Merck Pharmaceuticals and mom Ruthiabell took care of the home and kids—Rosey still worked, too. Only now he went to school, he opened his books and he studied hard, graduating from Roselle's Abraham Clark High School in 1951 to become the first member of his family to earn his high school diploma. It wasn't a big deal then in the Grier clan—none of his family members came to watch him graduate—but Rosey didn't

Rosey Grier played on both sides of the ball during his Penn State career, but it was his stout work along the defensive line that helped keep Illinois' vaunted ground game in check in the teams' 1954 season opener. Grier flourished further as a defensive lineman during 11 professional seasons.

need applause. After all, high school was just the beginning. And he knew it.

The Setting

As a high school senior, Grier received interest from several schools, and even went to visit Virginia State University. But it was Penn State's emphasis on academics that ultimately lured him to central Pennsylvania. Officially, he arrived on a track scholarship, with the understanding that he'd play football as well. The move saved an extra football scholarship for use by Rip Engle, who'd arrived in 1950 to coach the Nittany Lions.

"I'm at this place I'm not supposed to be," says Grier, who would go on to captain the Lions' track team in 1954 as a standout shot put, discus, and javelin thrower. "It's like, 'Okay, you did all that to get here. Now how you gonna stay here?'" It's a question he'd ask and answer time and time again in his life.

As a Penn State freshman, Grier's most pressing concern was what to study. He tried music first, seeing how he was a naturally talented singer. Thing is, he'd never actually read notes or studied keys before. Instruments? No experience. A professor handed him a cello, "and man," he says, "I tell you, I had a fit."

His grades slumped, and he wound up academically ineligible for spring track. So he changed course, switching to physical education and psychology and pulling his grades up in time for his sophomore football season in 1952. By then he was an entrenched member of a talented class that boasted the likes of Jesse Arnelle, Buddy Rowell, Sam Green, Don Bailey, and Jim Garrity. That year Grier also befriended just-arrived freshmen Charlie Blockson and Lenny Moore, who, along with Grier's class, would rejuvenate Penn State football.

Grier credits Engle and his staff—men like Joe Paterno, Frank Patrick, Jim O'Hora, J.T. White (hired in '54), and Sever "Papa Tor" Toretti—for his on-field growth. He loved and respected Engle, who never barked at him like some coaches who thought he'd play better with a more angry edge than his personality allowed. Grier, who also played on the offensive line throughout his time at State, learned the inner workings of playing the defensive front, like how to wait for blocks and set traps in pass rush. Toretti taught him how to spin off blocks and wrap up ball carriers, a skill he carried into the pros.

A bull rusher with speed off the ball—he'd played some fullback and run track relays in high school—Grier also began implementing a hand-to-the-helmet technique while he was an underclassman. He'd smack an offensive lineman's head to force him to move his body out of position, clearing his opening to the quarterback. (That move progressed in the pros thanks to Grier and the rest of the Rams' Fearsome Foursome of Deacon Jones, Merlin Olsen, and Lamar Lundy; the league eventually banned the technique.)

"It was fun, because I never felt that one guy could block me," Grier says. "You had to play a defensive scheme, but if I had the freedom to come off the ball, with my speed, I'd wreck a lot of plays."

Grier did his share of play disruption as Penn State went from 5-4 in 1951, with Grier starting as a freshman defensive tackle, to 7-2-1 in '52 and 6-3 in '53. With all the talent back on both sides of the ball, there were high hopes in Happy Valley for the 1954 season. Problem is, for the second consecutive season, the Nittany Lions had to open on the road against a Big Ten power. A season earlier it had been Wisconsin drubbing the Lions 20-0 in Madison, thanks largely to the running of fullback Alan Ameche, then a year shy of winning the Heisman. Now it was a trip to Champaign, Illinois, to grapple the Fighting Illini, who had shared the 1953 conference title with Michigan State. This time, the road team was better prepared.

The Game of My Life
By Rosey Grier

PENN STATE AT ILLINOIS
SEPTEMBER 25, 1954

I was up for All-American going into that year (1954) along with Lenny Moore. But I don't think I was motivated any more by that, because you play within who you are. See, I think the mistake a lot of people make is they try to play up to their publicity as opposed to playing who they are. And that's all I ever wanted to be, the best I could be.

We took a train out to Illinois, and we were very apprehensive about playing those guys. They were supposed to have the greatest backfield ever assembled in college: J.C. Caroline, Mickey Bates, and Abe Woodson. I know when we were training for the game they were talking about how great they were and how nobody was gonna be able to touch them—stuff like that. But we had an excellent defensive team, and we had a defense planned. The plan was to gang tackle. Everybody go to the ball. When the ball is in somebody's hands, don't stop 'til the whistle blows.

We went down in the game early, but there was no panic. When you play your game, if you're running your plays and doing what you're supposed to do, that's all you have to do. When you play within your own scheme and execute, you'll come out okay.

The game got physical because you had gang tackling. That means you're not going in there just touching someone. You're going in there popping. The one play I remember more than anything else is the play I got hurt on. It was kind of a fluky injury. I got hit almost after the play was over. We had made the tackle and then I got hurt.

The play had been off to my right. I was chasing the guy and my leg got blocked the wrong way. It was my left knee. I wasn't hurt very badly. You know, when you hurt your knee, you hurt your knee. If it gets stiff on you and swells up, it's hard to get ready to go the next time. I did stick in there, though, because when you're in a game and you're hot, you can keep going. The idea is to put ice on it, but we were out of town, so I didn't have the chance to put the ice on as I should have. The next game against Syracuse, I could only go straight on defense. I mean, I got better, but I wasn't what I was for a while. It was the beginning of really realizing that you could have an injury and it could bother you for a long time. That was also when I began to tape up my knees.

Anyway, we were able to contain that offensive backfield that day against Illinois, and that ultimately made the difference. It was a great accomplishment for us to win that game, especially since as great as they thought they were, you'd almost have thought they wouldn't have needed a line.

It was a big upset for us, but we didn't know how big cause it was early in the season. It was a win, but not time to celebrate. Still, the fact remained, for us to go out there and beat this team with all the publicity was a great coup. It made us feel really good. It was also a shock to them, cause they suddenly realized they were not invincible—and that they could be whipped.

Game Results

The September 25, 1954, season opener at Illinois would answer many questions that had brewed all summer. Could an underdog Penn State club from the East—different sources pitted the Illini as anywhere from 6-to-14-point favorites—defeat the class of the Big Ten, a consensus conference favorite entering the season? Was there any way to slow down Illinois' three-headed monster of a rushing attack, Caroline, Bates, and Woodson? Was the pride of Reading, Pennsylvania, Lenny Moore, in the same class of running backs as Caroline? After all, Caroline was an All-American who'd rushed for 1,256 yards in 1953, and he'd already surpassed several school rushing records previously held by the immortal Red Grange. Everything was answered in 60 minutes of game clock.

An ABC radio broadcast audience and 54,090 partisan fans listened and watched as the home team struck first. Penn State had won the toss and taken the opening drive to near midfield, but after State's starting quarterback, Bob Hoffman, was picked off, it took Illinois all of four plays—three rushes followed by a touchdown-scoring screen to Woodson—to jump on top. Caroline, though, missed the point-after attempt, and it was 6-0. That was key.

Penn State's defense, stubborn and relentless all afternoon, set up the Lions' first score late in the first quarter when Moore clobbered Bates, forcing a fumble that Arnelle recovered at the Illinois 28. After a Moore run, Don Bailey, inserted into the game at quarterback, connected with Arnelle racing across the goalline for a touchdown. Jim Garrity hit the extra point for a 7-6 Lions lead.

The physicality and drama continued. On one play, Grier stripped Illinois quarterback Em Lindbeck near midfield and Penn State recovered the fumble, but the Lions could not capitalize. Later in the second quarter, the deceptively quick Caroline broke free and might have scored save for a lunging ankle tackle by Moore. With less than three minutes left in the half, Penn State's Bailey kept the ball for 50 yards on an option. Two plays later he ran it again, but before being dragged down, the quarterback tossed a lateral to Moore, who raced in for the score to make it 14-6 State at halftime.

The Illini did not go quietly. In the third quarter Lindbeck found 227-pound end Charley Butler for a 36-yard completion, the longest pass play by either team that day. Three downs later Woodson galloped in from 17 yards, but another missed extra point kept it 14-12.

That's as close at it would get, though Illinois had opportunities. Moore snuffed out one fourth-quarter drive with a leaping interception at State's 48. Then, on its best opportunity in the final period, rather than risk a field goal on fourth-and-6 from Penn State's 16, Illinois handed to Caroline, who was mauled by Garrity and Frank Reich. As the final minutes ticked off, Penn State drove methodically downfield to kill the clock.

Evidence of the upset appeared in the game's box score. Caroline had gone for 116 yards on 20 carries, but his teammates netted just 39 yards combined. Meanwhile Moore (137 yards on 18 rushes) carried a State ground assault that gained 293 yards to Illinois' 157. State's powerful defense had forced two fumbles and an interception, and Grier's line dominance was the talk of the press box.

"You could spot his huge frame making tackles on both sides of the center," wrote Ridge Riley in the *Penn State Alumni News*. "How could a 245-pounder get around like that?"

Thousands of students greeted the triumphant Lions on their return to State College, and Engle told the throng it was the most satisfying coaching victory of his career. (Illinois, meanwhile, never recovered from the defeat, finishing 1-8 that season.) The Lions would win their next two, against Syracuse and Virginia, before dropping a 19-14 home game to West Virginia, the lone ranked opponent on that year's schedule. Penn State rebounded to win four of its last five for a

7-2 finish on the strength of Moore's running—he averaged eight yards a carry that year for 1,082 in all—and a defense that pitched two shutouts and allowed an average of 10.2 points per game.

Grier missed first-team All-America status, but he says he wasn't disappointed, considering the era. "Being a black ballplayer, if there was a white ballplayer up for the same thing, you weren't gonna get it," he says. "In 1954 I had a coach—not Rip—tell me they wanted to send me to the East-West Game, but they were only going to have so many black ballplayers. And since I was that odd player, I wasn't gonna get it. ... Black ballplayers always thought, 'I have to be one and a half times better than the white ballplayer in order for me to get it.'"

Grier did help the '54 college all-stars beat the NFL-champion Cleveland Browns, and then to no surprise, he was drafted by the New York Giants. Grier expected New York to take him because when pro teams had sent him questionnaires, he'd written that he would only play for the Giants, hoping to stay close to his family. He played two years for the Giants, returning to Penn State in the interim to finish his degree work. He joined the Army for one year in 1957, then continued suiting up for Big Blue until he was traded to the Los Angeles Rams in 1963.

"I wasn't happy about it at all," he says of the Giants trading him, "but you either go with the trade or you quit. And I wasn't ready to quit."

Reflecting on State

As it was, Grier was just getting started in L.A., where he's lived since the trade in 1963. While still playing for the Rams, he went on his first acting audition, landing a part in the show *The Man From U.N.C.L.E.* The role launched a lengthy performing career that included extensive work on TV (*Daniel Boone; Movin' On; Roots: The Next Generations*), in movies (*The Glove, Rabbit Test, The Thing with Two Heads*), and myriad guest TV appearances (*The Simpsons, The Love Boat, Kojak, I Dream of Jeannie*).

Grier attributes his comfort in public speaking forums to acting, "because it made you do something outside of yourself," he says. "You had to learn the lines and make them you." In the late 1960s, he used those abilities when asked to speak in support of Robert Kennedy's presidential campaign. Grier even once subbed in for Kennedy at a speaking engagement, whom he'd befriended at a Washington fundraiser. And he was with Kennedy in Los Angeles in 1968 when the Democratic candidate was assassinated by Palestinian militant Sirhan Sirhan.

"When shots rang out," recalls Grier, "I came running up, and there were people grappling with this guy who had a gun. So I went and caught him by his legs and put him up on this table. George Plimpton had the gun hand, so I put my hand over the gun and Plimpton's hand and wrenched the gun out of Sirhan's hand. Later I had the gun in my pocket, and I gave it to Rafer Johnson to turn in."

Grier was devastated by Kennedy's death—"It seemed I died with him," he once said—and spent years helping the family whenever it needed something. "I guess I was trying to make up for their loss."

Grier has lived many lives since. Aside from the acting, he once sang in a quartet at New York's Carnegie Hall (second tenor), he's recorded albums (including one with Bobby Darin) and written books, one about his needlepoint hobby (he says he no longer knits). Through his adventures, he's always given back, working with kids through a celebrity group called Teammates, volunteering with the Junior Olympics for mentally retarded children, and becoming president of Giant Step, an organization set up to aid children and senior citizens. In the midst of such work, he also began searching for his true identity.

"One day I'm helping gang kids, bailing 'em out of jail, going to burials and courts, talking to these kids about how they're living their lives," he says. "It dawned on me, I was no different from them. My life was as disjointed as theirs. I wasn't sure why I was doing all these things, what they really meant."

While Rosey searched for Rosey, he found God, and by living according to God's rules, he says it gave his life new meaning. He became ordained as a minister in 1985 and remarried wife Margie, whom he'd divorced "because I felt she was the one that was messing me up," he says. The couple's still married, and they have a son together, Rosey Jr.

Grier also has a daughter, Cheryl, four grandchildren, and three great-grandchildren. He now spends much of his time in his community affairs role with the Milken Family Foundation, speaking to kids and honoring standout teachers. Fall weekends, he'll still pull up in front of the tube to watch Penn State football. And though he hasn't been back to State College in several years, he remains tight with teammates Lenny Moore and Charlie Blockson.

Above all else, he holds fast to one thing from college. "The team concept—it's the concept I use today, that everybody is on the same team," he says. "And we all have a part to play on that team, so don't think of yourself as being unimportant. If you take that team and transfer it over to the real world, it's the same thing. It's not their world—it's our world. And you have a part to play in that world."

Another winning role for Grier.

3

GALEN HALL

NAME: Galen Sam Hall
BORN: August 14, 1940, in Altoona, Pennsylvania
HOMETOWN: Williamsburg, Pennsylvania
CURRENT RESIDENCE: State College, Pennsylvania
OCCUPATION: Offensive coordinator/running backs coach,
Penn State University
POSITION: Quarterback
HEIGHT: 5 feet, 9 inches
PLAYING WEIGHT: 185 pounds
YEARS LETTERED: 1959 to 1961
NUMBER WORN AT PSU: 25
ACCOMPLISHMENTS: Two-year starter at Penn State won
Gator Bowl MVP honors in 1961, his senior season; set a
school record with 256-yard passing day against Pitt in '61;
named to all-time Penn State team in 1967 by *Pittsburgh Press*
editor Chet Smith; played two seasons in NFL; tabbed 1984
Associated Press Coach of the Year while head coach at the
University of Florida; has also served as an NFL assistant and
NFL Europe head coach
THE GAME: The Liberty Bowl, Penn State versus Alabama,
December 19, 1959

The Young Life of Galen Hall

In the fall of 1957, when Galen Hall was considering where he wanted to play college football, his thoughts turned directly to his family. And for good reason: He was very close to his immediate family, which had hung together through trying times. Hall's father, Galen Sr., a football coach at Warrior's Mark High School in Huntingdon County, Pennsylvania, had been killed in a car accident in the spring of 1940. His mother, Grace, then six months pregnant with their first child, was also in the car, but she survived the wreck and Galen was born three months later. Grace, who never remarried, took Galen to live with her father, Joseph Westbrook, in his large home in Williamsburg. Galen's aunt, uncle, and cousin, Joseph Harper, also resided there.

Galen spent his entire youth living at his grandfather's place, listening to baseball games by radio and idolizing Stan Musial and later Roberto Clemente. Grace worked as a teacher 25 miles away in Claysburg, leaving Galen with plenty of time to mimic his heroes and develop his own skills, some with guidance from older cousin Joe (five years his senior), others honed while playing with neighborhood buddies.

"Football, basketball, baseball," Hall says. "Those are the only three sports we had. No track or anything like that. It was a very small community, and very much behind the athletic programs in the high school."

Hall looked up to those ahead of him at the high school level, and when he arrived there, he made the most of it, leading Williamsburg to an undefeated campaign and district title his senior year. That fall of 1957, Penn State assistant coach Joe Paterno drove to Williamsburg—a town of fewer than 1,500 residents consuming half a square mile in land area—to watch Hall and the Pirates, but Hall turned an ankle early in the game. Paterno returned a separate time to watch Hall play basketball, then began aggressively recruiting the three-sport athlete.

Hall had other options to consider. He made recruiting visits to USC and Michigan State, and received interest from several more programs. Alternately, he had potential as a baseball prospect. He even flirted with spurning the gridiron for the diamond and a minor league contract.

Hall ultimately chose college football and head coach Rip Engle's Penn State program. But it wasn't the prestige of playing for a national power that swayed Hall, who had grown up an Oklahoma fan. Between 1950-57, Penn State amassed a pedestrian 47-23-3 record and finished in the final Associated Press Top 20 poll only once—No. 20 in 1954. While traditional powers Oklahoma, Notre Dame, Ohio State, and Tennessee garnered national attention and broadcasts, Penn State remained stuck in the "minor leagues" stereotype that pervaded Eastern football.

Still, after meeting with Penn State's staff and touring University Park in the spring of 1957, Hall chose proximity over all else. "I visited a few places, but I wanted to stay close to home for my grandfather, mother, and family to see me play," Hall says. "I respected Joe and Rip very much, and that was a plus. But I still think the family had a lot to do with it."

The Setting

Hall's college career began inauspiciously in 1958. Upon joining Penn State's freshman team that fall, he immediately had problems taking snaps. "For some reason, I just couldn't hang onto the football," he says. "I played very sparingly. I was the third quarterback cause there weren't four."

He found himself buried on Engle's depth chart when winter arrived. But something happened in the off-season before Hall joined the varsity squad as a sophomore: He somehow cured his problems handling the pigskin. It's a turnaround he today categorizes as nothing short of remarkable. Part of it grew from the faith Paterno, Hall's position coach and a former quarterback himself, showed in the young signal-caller. Hall took it from there.

The coaching staff staged a quarterback competition in spring practice 1959, and Hall impressed, beating out Allen Brewster and Jon Lang to become starter Richie Lucas' backup entering the '59 season.

In those years Engle utilized a "Reddie" offense, a complete second-team unit that spelled the first-teamers, and not just at mop-up time. Engle would often employ Lucas and the starters for eight minutes a quarter, then trot out Hall and the "Reddies" to finish the period.

"If we were driving in, they'd keep Richie in," says Hall, who doubled as a safety on defense that season. "They protected themselves that way; they didn't put that much on me. But I was fortunate I got enough playing time to get some experience."

Engle's two-platoon attack bred quality depth on his roster, which already boasted a strong senior class headed by Lucas and a slew of senior linemen: Charlie Janerrette (second-team All-American that year), Andy Stynchula, Tom Mulraney, and Norm Neff to name a few. It also gave underclassmen time to cozy up to a run-and-shoot brand of offense considered innovative for its era. "We had double slots, outside belly, some tight end plays, stuff like that," Hall says. "Every time we see the double slot or spread formation now, Joe [Paterno] brings it up that back then we were in the same formations, throwing in the flat and the curls behind it."

With a wide-open attack and multiple contributors on both sides of the ball, the Lions rolled to 7-0 in '59, including road wins against Army and West Virginia. Lucas, tabbed "Riverboat Richie" by the Penn State sports information department for his daring play-calling—and to boost his Heisman buzz—was the team's star. The eventual Maxwell Award winner and Heisman Trophy runner-up led Penn State in total offense that season, becoming State's first All-American since Harry "Lighthorse" Wilson in 1923.

Yet even Lucas' abilities weren't enough to keep Penn State from remaining unbeaten in a late-season home clash with Syracuse, then No. 1 in the nation and the eventual national champ. The Lions rallied from a 20-6 deficit that day but were denied a tie when Roger Kochman was stuffed on a two-point conversion with five minutes remaining in the game.

Penn State stumbled again in the season finale, 22-7 to Pitt, a defeat some pinned on low team morale surrounding a previous announcement that win or lose, State was headed to the Liberty Bowl in Philadelphia. While players pined for the Orange, Sugar, Cotton, or Gator bowls, Liberty organizers had convinced some college officials that an in-state bowl appearance would serve a positive financial purpose for the city and state, thus making it a plus for the state university. PSU's players voted to play in Philly, but many later said the Liberty Bowl was the only option offered.

Still, despite the letdown against Pitt, Penn State received good news when, unable to land Georgia or Georgia Tech, Liberty organizers learned Alabama coach Bear Bryant was willing to bring his team north for the game. Suddenly Penn State had a one-loss opponent worth getting pumped for.

The Game of My Life
By Galen Hall

THE LIBERTY BOWL
PENN STATE VERSUS ALABAMA
DECEMBER 19, 1959

The '59 team was a pretty good football team. We had some big linemen—Stynchula, Janerrette, and Richie, obviously. They were all seniors and you looked up to them. Roger Kochman, Bill Saul, and Jay Huffman were all sophomores in my class who played. We played a lot of people.

Despite starting 7-0, we weren't disappointed to finish 8-2. There might have been some who felt that way, but here we are as sophomores—Roger, Bill, Jay, myself—and we're fortunate to be playing. We're just happy to be playing anywhere. A bowl's a bowl, whether it's in Philadelphia or wherever else.

I recall staying around State College during finals that year and scrimmaging up there. We were playing Alabama, and I remember Joe getting us in and showing us film. They were really good on defense and were tough and physical. So we knew it would be a good challenge for us. As for Coach Bryant, he was a national, prominent figure then, but as a 19-year-old sophomore, I didn't revere him the way I do today.

Galen Hall's (No. 25) touchdown pass off a fake field goal was the only scoring in the 1959 Liberty Bowl. Two years later the quarterback won Gator Bowl MVP honors in his final college game.

As the story goes, Rip came in and wanted a fake field goal for the game. He was going to put it in; we hadn't used it earlier in the year. Now, we didn't put it in until I believe the Thursday before we played on Saturday. So we didn't practice it until Thursday, and as I recall, I didn't practice it at all. We ran it twice in practice and Richie took both snaps.

Back then you went out and expected a tough, physical game all the time. And that's exactly what we got with Alabama. Neither of us were that good on offense. I mean, we were good on offense, but we had two good defenses going together, and we were fortunate enough to throw that screen pass right before halftime.

Richie had gotten hurt ... in the second quarter, and I played the rest of it. I don't think I was nervous. I think you just go out, you get hit, you start reacting, and you go play. And of course, after Richie got hurt, I had to run that fake field goal. I don't remember every detail about the play, but I know I rolled out and threw it back, and thank God Roger [Kochman] was where he was supposed to be. We completed it, he scored, and I was thinking, "Boy, am I lucky."

Not that as players we ever thought one touchdown would be enough. We thought we'd go score again. But the way the game unfolded, we were lucky enough to play good enough defense that they didn't score. If you go back to the stats, our defense was dominant.

Anytime you do something that's good and win a football game, you're very happy about it. This was the first Liberty Bowl, and Penn State hadn't been to a bowl game in a while (11 years). So getting to that bowl game and winning it, I think that started us thinking, "Hey, we're gonna go to bowl games." And we were fortunate enough to go to a couple more in my time there.

Game Results

Penn State had home-state advantage in the inaugural Liberty Bowl, but it didn't stop the media from latching on to Bear Bryant, who a year earlier had signed a 10-year deal to become football coach and athletic director at his alma mater, saying he'd "heard mama calling." The pregame attention following Alabama's coach peeved Paterno, who felt his head coach, Rip Engle, wasn't receiving the same level of pub. "I was all, 'We'll show you, you son of a … ,'" Paterno said. By the time the game ended and postgame festivities concluded, Paterno and his colleagues would develop a genuine appreciation for Bryant's sportsmanship as a coach.

First, though, the Lions, appearing in just their third bowl in school history, had to find a way to score on No. 10 Alabama's defense. The Tide gave up 17 points in a season-opening loss to Georgia that fall, then didn't allow more than seven points in a game the rest of the way, pitching four shutouts to finish the regular season 7-1-2.

Penn State, 12th in the Associated Press poll entering the bowl, was nearly as stingy. The Lions, with size up front and speed in the secondary—led by Lucas, Ed Caye, Jim Kerr, and Jack Urban, State picked off 22 passes that season—posted two shutouts and held all but three opponents to 12 or fewer points. On December 19, in 42-degree weather dominated by 20-mile-per-hour winds, the defensive war was on.

Playing before a seemingly small crowd of 36,211 fans— Philadelphia's Municipal Stadium, later renamed JFK Stadium, held 100,000 spectators at the time—Alabama posed the first serious scoring threat, driving to Penn State's 27-yard line in the first quarter. That's the closest the Tide would come to State's end zone all day. Penn State responded offensively, with Lucas collecting a quick 55 yards on nine carries. But early in the second quarter, he left the game with a badly bruised hip and did not return.

In came Hall. After Huffman recovered a fumble at Alabama's 28 (each team would lose four fumbles in the game), State drove to set up first-and-goal at the 5-yard line. Bama's defense, though, stiffened, batting down Hall's pass attempt to Bob Mitinger in the end zone and forcing a turnover on downs.

After an Alabama drive went nowhere, the wind knocked down a Tide punt, setting up State at Bama's 19. But that drive too proved fruitless when Sam Stellatella's field goal attempt from the 12 was blocked. Then it happened again: A short Bama drive forced a helpless punt into the gusts, giving State a first down at Alabama's 22. This time, with seconds running out in the half, Engle called for a fake field goal, a play he'd inserted after watching film and detecting a flaw in the Tide's kick rush. The Lions faked it and Hall threw to fullback Pat Botula, but it gained only 4 yards. Now at the 18, the Lions hurriedly lined up for a 25-yard field goal. But the fake was on again. Hall, the holder, took the snap and rolled right, feigning interest in receiver Norm Neff. As Bama's defenders rushed to blanket Neff, Hall whirled and hit Kochman on the left sideline. With four blockers leading the way and a late comeback block by Neff, Kochman broke it for an 18-yard score. Stellatella's point after made it 7-0 PSU at the break.

"You never know," Paterno said. "If you told us before the game that a fake screen pass would have won it, we wouldn't have believed it. Except for one guy: The boss."

The one-touchdown margin stuck, as both defenses ruled the second half. Penn State allowed just 111 yards rushing and 27 passing for the game, while the Lions posted 315 yards of total offense. "I think we were very fortunate we weren't beaten by four or five touchdowns," Bryant told the *Philadelphia Inquirer* after Bama's 7-0 setback. "Penn State outhit us, outsmarted us, outblocked us, outtackled us, and outcoached us."

Bryant reiterated those sentiments at a post-bowl banquet. "Johnny Carson was the entertainment, and Ed McMahon was there," Paterno said, "but I was most impressed by how gracious Paul Bryant was after a tough loss. All he talked about was what a terrific job Rip had done.

"I also admired him because he'd bring his team up north. We could never get Tennessee to do that. That was also the first time Alabama ever played against a black kid—Charlie Janerrette, a Philly kid—and [Bryant] was bound to take some flak. Unless you're stupid, you learn from people like Bryant."

Hall certainly gained from the experience. The kid Engle labeled "a coach on the field" made sure the momentum from 1959 never dissipated. In 1960, the year State moved from 30,000-seat Beaver Field on the west side of campus to all-steel Beaver Stadium on the east end of campus—the structure was disassembled and moved in 700 pieces, with 16,000 additional seats added to the venue—Hall carried the Lions to a 7-3 record and a return to the Liberty Bowl. They dispatched Oregon 41-12 in that one, and a year later, with help from 1,000-yard rusher Kochman, State went 8-3, thumping Georgia Tech 30-15 in the Gator Bowl.

"Georgia Tech probably thought they were gonna beat us," says Hall, who went 12 of 22 for 175 yards and three touchdowns to win MVP of the game, his last as a college quarterback. "That's the year we couldn't stay in Jacksonville on account of Dave Robinson. So we had a hotel situation, racial issues, and to go down to the South and defeat them was very satisfying for everybody."

Said the always-frank Paterno that year of his outgoing senior quarterback: "You try to evaluate Hall as a pro quarterback or for All-

American and he doesn't stand a chance. Yet he's invaluable to a college football team."

Nevertheless, Hall's Gator Bowl performance boosted his stock, as did his big day in one of the year's senior bowls, when he topped 300 yards passing for an all-star team coached by then-Washington Redskins coach Bill McPeak. The timely success landed Hall a free-agent deal as a backup with the Redskins in 1962. In '63 he signed with Weeb Ewbank and the Jets, seeing action in 13 games and throwing for three touchdowns.

By then Hall was satisfied with his brief taste of pro ball. His goal was to coach, and with help from Engle and Paterno, he landed his first assistant's gig under Gene Corum at West Virginia in 1964. It was the start of a lifetime spent teaching the game he loves.

Reflecting on State

Hall's done it all since his playing days ended in 1963. From West Virginia, Hall—again with assists from Paterno and Engle—landed on Jim Mackenzie's staff at Oklahoma. Over the next 18 seasons Hall helped the Sooners win 161 games and two national titles, parlaying that success into a job at Florida, where he was promoted to head coach after an NCAA investigation forced out Charley Pell. Hall won AP national coach of the year in 1984 for directing the Gators to a 9-1-1 season, but ironically, five years later, he too was felled by an NCAA investigation (sparked by an internal investigation conducted by university attorneys). A 1990 NCAA report listed two violations, including payment to cover a player's child support bill.

"I have great, fond memories of Florida, and I still love the Gators and the Gator people," says Hall, whom Paterno hired back to Penn State as a grad assistant in 1990. "It's just a couple people that I have a hard time dealing with, and that will always remain."

Hall has only enriched and diversified his coaching résumé in the last decade and a half. He's coached in the XFL (Orlando Rage), World League (Orlando Thunder), NFL Europe (Rhein Fire), and even returned to the NFL as running backs coach for the Dallas Cowboys. He and wife Elaine were set to rejoin the NFL Europe circuit in 2004 when Paterno called to offer him the offensive coordinator job at Penn State vacated by Fran Ganter, who was leaving to become Penn State's associate athletic director for football administration.

"You always respect Joe for what he's done for college football and what he stands for and what he did for me," Hall says. "So Penn State is the only place I would have come back to college football for. I wouldn't have gone anywhere else as an assistant coach in college."

As it is, the father of five returned to his Penn State family, "back here in the hills," he says, and within two years he had Penn State back atop the Big Ten standings. His pilgrimage to State College 42 years after graduation has sparked old memories and connected him with old friends, like members of the 1959 team who in 2004 were feted on the 45th anniversary of Penn State's first bowl win.

"There were about 30 of us there, but we've lost a couple of them since then," he says. "It was good to see people. My travels took me to Oklahoma and Florida all those years, so I really hadn't kept in close touch with any of them.

"This is a great place, a great school, and I'm working for a great person," he adds with a nod to Paterno, who recruited him so many falls ago. "Hopefully we can keep this thing going the way Penn State would want it to go."

4

LENNY MOORE

NAME: Leonard Edward Moore
BORN: November 25, 1933, in Reading, Pennsylvania
HOMETOWN: Reading, Pennsylvania
CURRENT RESIDENCE: Randallstown, Maryland
OCCUPATION: Intervention and prevention program specialist,
    Maryland Department of Education; retired NFL player
POSITION: Halfback, defensive back
HEIGHT: 6 feet
PLAYING WEIGHT: 195 pounds
YEARS LETTERED: 1953 to 1955
NUMBER WORN AT PSU: 42
ACCOMPLISHMENTS: Topped 1,000 all-purpose yards in each
    of his three seasons at Penn State; finished career with 3,543
    all-purpose yards; had 12 100-yard rushing games as a
    Nittany Lion; first-round pick (ninth overall) by Baltimore
    Colts in 1956 was also Penn State's first NFL first-round draft
    choice; won 1956 NFL Rookie of the Year; five-time All-Pro
    helped Colts win 1958 NFL championship and completed 12-
    year pro career with 12,393 net yards (5,175 rushing) and
    113 TDs; inducted into Pro Football Hall of Fame in 1975.
THE GAME: Penn State versus Syracuse, November 5, 1955

The Young Life of Lenny Moore

Lenny Moore remembers details of his youth that don't sound pleasant. There were months the Moores spent on welfare, the days they slept at Reading's Hope Rescue Mission awaiting housing, Cream of Wheat breakfasts, and pot of cabbage dinners. But when Moore peers back 60 years into his past, he somehow sees and feels nothing but love. And for that he credits his parents.

"My mind never reflected on what little we had or didn't have, because happiness was there," he says. "I'll never forget, in elementary school, I couldn't wait to get home, because that's where the love was. [I'd] come home, 'Hi Mom! How you doing? What are you doing? Where's Pops at?' 'Well, you know, he's still working. He'll be home later on.' Just happy, man. I often think about that even now."

Lenny's mother, Virginia, had been married once before, but her first husband died young. She later met and married George Moore, and the union ultimately resulted in a family of 12 kids, with as many as eight living together at one time. Lenny spent most of his childhood in Reading, save for a few years in Brooklyn, New York, where his father George had found work. It was on the move back from New York that the Moores stayed at the mission while seeking housing.

George worked a number of jobs during Lenny's youth, including one with a railroad crew and another as a burner with American Chain and Cable. Unbeknownst to Lenny, his dad was also illiterate. Only later, with Lenny at Penn State, did George learn to read and write (Virginia taught him), which helped him learn how to install indoor plumbing in place of the outhouse Lenny had grown up with at home. "I didn't know until years later when my older sister said, 'Did you know your father couldn't read?'" Moore says. "It was almost like, you can do anything you put your mind to."

Despite the obvious presence of parental inspiration, Moore never felt compelled to commit to his studies in his years at Northeast Junior High and Reading High School. He passed his classes, but forget A's. He simply got by. Money was tight, so his older brothers had joined the Army, sending allotment checks home to help pay bills. Lenny figured he'd do the same when the time came.

Long before his Hall of Fame career with the Baltimore Colts, Lenny Moore starred as a speedy two-way player at Penn State. And he was at his best when Jim Brown's Syracuse Orangemen came calling in 1955.

He loved football, but college ball never entered his mind. And rightfully so. Not until Reading's first-string running back quit the team in Moore's junior season did he even begin to regularly carry the ball. Only then, when word got out about the speedy back, did scholarship offers begin arriving on Coach Andy Stopper's desk. Stopper believed in Moore and spoke to him about his potential. He motivated the teen to pursue an educational and athletic plan that in 1952 took him to Penn State, where he became the first of his 12 siblings to attend college.

The Setting

"The place then, as it is now, was breathtaking," recalls Moore of his first impression of Penn State. Still, as a frosh in '52 who had never been away from home, he grew homesick fast: "I wanted to be on every bus heading back," he says. Time helped. Moore befriended classmates, even though most were white. He formed a strong bond with Charlie Blockson, an African-American teammate and Moore's freshman year roommate. Blockson was from Norristown, and his high school track and football teams had competed against Moore's at Reading.

In 1953, Moore was paired with a new roommate, Jesse Arnelle, a powerful lineman and All-American basketball player. Arnelle would co-captain the 1954-55 PSU hoops team to what remains the lone Final Four appearance in school history, and years later he became head of the university's board of trustees. "Mr. Everything" on the field, in the classroom, and on campus, he was an older role model for Moore.

In addition, Moore benefited from a warm relationship with coach Rip Engle. "I loved him—*luvvvvvved* him," Moore says. "He was the epitome of what you hope all coaches would be like. Not only was he a gentleman and a good coach, but his personality created an atmosphere where you just wanted to play for Rip.

"Paterno was a holler guy. But it was a good balance for Rip. Rip wouldn't curse, and if he did, he'd say, 'Oh, I'm sorry. Forgive me. I didn't mean to say that.' You could not help but love the man, because he carried himself the same way every time you saw him. ... It gave me a lot of confidence, because when things would throw me off, I'd get to thinking about Rip, and that brought me back on key."

Surrounded by a new family of coaches and teammates, Moore found his game. He saw a lot of action in 1953, demonstrating big-play ability, like a 64-yard touchdown run at Wisconsin in the season opener that was nullified by a motion penalty. "In Leonard Moore,

Penn State has a menace," wrote Leo Riordan in the *Philadelphia Inquirer.* "Moore is overdue, and future opponents will get it."

By the close of his sophomore year, the "Reading Express," as Moore was known, had ridden Engle's split-T offense to the tune of 601 rushing yards, the most by any Penn State back in one season since Fran Rogel 15 years earlier. He was also developing another nickname, "Spats," for the way he'd tape his ankles atop his high-top shoes.

Engle didn't allow players then to wear low-cut shoes. When Moore once saw fellow back Bob Pollard taping his injured ankle outside his high-top shoe, he began doing the same. Even in practice he'd do it, using tape from the ends of spools so as not to get in trouble for draining supplies. Moore adjusted the tape's tightness around his Riddells to create a snug feel. He continued the routine throughout his years at State and into the pros, when he'd practice in high-tops and switch to lightweight, thin-soled Adidas shoes for game day. "I strapped those boys down," he says.

"Spats" had some memorable days as an underclassman. During his sophomore year, Moore took a draw play and danced 70 yards to pay dirt in a win against rival Pitt. Earlier in '53, the two-way player (like many teammates at the time) proved his skill as a defensive back by picking off a pass to seal a win against Syracuse. He was shoved hard out of bounds after that play, igniting a brawl at Beaver Stadium that symbolized the ferocity of the era's 'Cuse-State rivalry.

"I was on the ground, and a couple guys from Syracuse jumped on me," Moore says of the '53 melee. "I worked my way loose and stood off to the side where I could see what the heck was going on. I saw people swinging and kicking. I kept my eyes open to make sure nobody came up behind me to get me."

The next year, as a junior, Moore went for 120 yards and two scores against Virginia. He made history that season by becoming the first black athlete to play a college football game in Forth Worth, Texas, rushing for 109 yards and a score at TCU. "I guess," Arnelle said of what made Moore such a talented runner, "it's because Lenny just doesn't like to be tackled."

A week after the TCU contest, Penn State played its first nationally televised game, a road tilt versus Penn, and Moore hushed the Quakers faithful with 143 yards and three touchdowns in a 35-13 blowout. "Spindle-legged Lenny Moore," penned Herb Good in the *Philadelphia Inquirer*, "a hot rod in football togs, ran wild on Franklin Field."

With his ability, Moore's senior year seemed to carry limitless potential—except that it almost never happened. Poor grades led to Moore's expulsion from school in 1955. Admittedly young and immature, Moore and his girlfriend at the time considered eloping and leaving State College. But he would have needed a job and a place to live, neither of which he had. He had no plan.

He did, however, have Coach Stopper from Reading, a friend who never stopped looking out for Moore. He also had Engle and his coaching staff, who convinced Moore to stay in University Park for summer classes. He enrolled in the extra session and landed a part-time job weighing trucks in an asphalt plant. By August '55, he'd straightened out his grades and earned enough credits to regain full-time admission for fall semester.

Still, even with Moore in uniform, a team that was 7-2 in '54 struggled for identity in '55 with senior linemen like Arnelle and Rosie Grier departed. Teams keyed on Moore; Navy held him to just 37 yards on 18 carries in a 34-14 defeat of the Lions. Penn State was just 3-3 when Syracuse came to town riding the powerful legs of one James Nathaniel Brown, a junior at the time. The battle of the backs was on.

The Game of My Life
By Lenny Moore

PENN STATE VERSUS SYRACUSE
NOVEMBER 5, 1955

I think people thought more about my matchup with Jim Brown after the game than before. Jim had an odd style about him. It wasn't really a different style, but he polished it. He wasn't a flashy tailback.

Not at all. And it wasn't that he just automatically ran over people. Somehow he spliced some of that together—the way he would lean or the way he would move. He'd do a sort of sidestep thing to get away from people, but he was so strong with his straight arm and things. He had all of that polished to the point where we were saying, "Damn, is this the same guy we saw last year? This can't be the same guy."

Tackling him, it was just like hitting a solid wall. You had to figure out where you wanted to hit him. My thing was to go low, cause I didn't want those big thighs crushing at me, and I didn't want him to get that forearm in there. So I figured I gotta go in there from the knees down to try to pull him down.

Anyway, that day we were down 13-0, because (Brown) had missed an extra point. We got a touchdown right before halftime and it was 13-7. Then they went up 20-7. That was tough, because … we couldn't turn the ball over. Their team was steady. They're gonna move the ball and we gotta stop them or hold them any way we can.

We made it 20-14. After that I was thinking, don't fumble this ball. You don't want to make any mistakes. So you're being cautious. Then again, you gotta be explosive at the same time. Still at 20-14, they started pushing to go all the way down the field. They were on like the 13-yard line, and Milt Plum grabbed an interception off Eddie Albright. Eddie was their quarterback; he had also been my quarterback in high school.

Then we mounted a drive. I don't remember much, other than the things that led up to it. But we always thought we had a chance to win. We looked a little shaky there for a while, but when we mounted that drive, we went all the way down. Don't make any mistakes; hold onto the ball. I remember Milt kicking the extra point, cause you know, Milt was no great kicker. He was a quarterback. But boom, right on through.

I remember Rip saying this was one of the greatest games that we've played in his coaching career, because he said each team gave so much, and for it to end up with us winning 21-20 had to be one of the best games of his coaching career.

I also remember that after the game, after we'd showered and left the locker room, I saw Jim. We started talking, and I congratulated him for a great game and wished him the best in his career. Hey, I'll tell ya, Jim was everything that people say he was. He was that good.

Game Results

It's no wonder that in the game's aftermath, the headlines told of a battle between two great rushers. It was just that. Brown struck first. With 30,321 fans plus a CBS regional TV audience watching, he took advantage of an early Penn State turnover, carrying five straight times and scoring on a fourth-down play. Syracuse, ranked 18th nationally and second in Eastern polls behind Navy, led 7-0. It hadn't defeated the Lions in State College since 1934. Would this be the day?

Later in the first half, Brown capped a 68-yard drive with a 5-yard touchdown catch from Albright. Some say Brown, also the Orangemen kicker, missed the ensuing point-after attempt that would have made it 14-0. Other accounts claim Penn State defensive end Jack Farls blocked the kick. Either way, the failed kick turned out to be the margin of victory.

State got another break with less than a minute left in the first half when linebacker Joe Sabol picked off an errant Albright pass in Syracuse territory and weaved to the 10. Seconds later, Plum hit Billy Kane for a score. But the good vibes State enjoyed at the break vanished when Brown took the opening kickoff of the second half to near midfield, tripped up by Moore's ankle tackle. Six plays later, Brown went around right end for a score and 20-7 lead.

The Lions answered right back, driving 59 yards—including a 20-yard pass to Kane—to make it 20-14 on Moore's 2-yard plunge. That's where the score remained for the rest of the third quarter and much of the fourth. Late in the game, Plum saved a touchdown by stopping Brown at State's 13-yard line after a 42-yard rumble. A Syracuse score on that drive would have effectively ended matters, but Plum produced again, pilfering an Albright pass in the end zone to quash the threat.

With six minutes left, Penn State began a frenetic drive. The Lions bulled 80 yards—Moore gained 45 of them on the ground, including a 22-yarder—and Plum sneaked in from 1 yard out to tie it. Plum's line-drive extra point cleared the crossbar by inches, and a Syracuse fumble on the next possession closed the chapter.

Brown went home with 159 yards, having scored all 20 Syracuse points. Moore rolled up 146 yards and a touchdown on 22 carries. Wrote Carl Hughes of the *Pittsburgh Press*: "Moore came up with an old-time performance when it was needed most. In Coach Rip Engle's jubilant words, 'Lenny never in his life was greater.'"

Reflecting on State

Despite many great days in blue and white, Moore's PSU teams never secured a bowl berth, and he never made first-team All-American—hard to imagine considering the Hall of Fame career that ensued. But a half-century later, Moore, who left State College a few credits shy of a degree—he hasn't returned to complete it—isn't bitter about what could have been perceived a snub. He points to the lack of media coverage Penn State received in the 1950s as an Eastern school with no league affiliation.

Moore's abilities blossomed with the Baltimore Colts. The flanker-halfback played inspired ball until 1967, earning MVP honors by player vote in 1964 and stringing together 18 consecutive games with at least one touchdown from 1963-65, a league record tied in 2005 by San Diego's LaDainian Tomlinson. His 113 career touchdowns remain ninth on the NFL's all-time list.

After retirement he tried broadcasting, working as an analyst for CBS alongside Frank Gifford. He was released after just one season, though to this day he's yet to receive an explanation why. "Every producer and director said I was doing exactly what needed to be done," he says, still genuinely miffed.

Moore went on to run marketing campaigns for Philadelphia agency NW Ayer & Son. Five years later, Colts GM Joe Thomas hired him for a community relations job at a $30,000 salary, more than he ever made in one year as a player. He stayed there until the team left Baltimore in 1983, since which he's worked for the Maryland State Department of Juvenile Justice, counseling kids (mostly middle school-aged) about staying out of trouble and how to build successful lives.

The Pro Football Hall of Famer spends much of his free time raising money for a scholarship fund named after his son Leslie, who passed away in 2001 from scleroderma, a systemic disease marked by thickened fibrous tissue. Since his death, the Leslie Moore Scholarship Fund has sent five Baltimore-area kids to college each year. "My son was my main man," says Lenny, who lives in Randallstown, Maryland, a suburb of Baltimore. "That's what keeps us rejuvenated."

Moore also draws sustenance from fans who still recognize him. And even after all these years, he's quick to acknowledge what others did for him to help him reach great heights. People like his parents, whom he had always hoped to send on a nice vacation, but never had the chance before his mother's death in 1958. Or Andy Stopper, his coach, friend, and confidante, whom Moore credits with being "the guy who showed me what it's like being a white guy in racial situations."

Then there's Rip Engle, who died in 1983 in a State College convalescent home. "I went back to see Rip in his last days," Moore says. "He was in a wheelchair, kind of slumped over. I stuck my head in and said, 'Hey man, how you doing?' I said, 'Do you know who I am?' He said, 'Lenny, how could I forget?' I said, 'I'm not gonna keep you, I just had to come and see you.' And he said, 'Thank you. Thank you.' I grabbed his hand and held it, then reached down and hugged him.' Then we left. Shortly after that he passed on."

In Moore's eyes, much of Engle lives on in Paterno, which is why Moore was humbled nearly to tears several years back when Paterno told Moore he was the best all-around player he'd ever coached. "Man, I almost hit the floor," says Moore, who in 2005 released an autobiography titled, *All Things Being Equal.* "He put his arms up and hugged me around the neck. He said, 'I mean it.' He emphasized that. I said, 'Joe, when I walk out of here, I don't know which way I'm going.'"

"I had good people in my life," Moore adds. "No telling where I would be if I didn't have those folks. They were there for me. Case closed."

5

JOE PATERNO

NAME: Joseph Vincent Paterno
BORN: December 21, 1926, in Flatbush, New York
DIED: January 22, 2012, State College, Pennsylvania
HOMETOWN: Brooklyn, New York
OCCUPATION: Head football coach, Penn State University
POSITION: Quarterback/defensive back, Brown University
YEARS AT PENN STATE: 1950 to 2012
ACCOMPLISHMENTS: One of two major college coaches (Amos
   Alonzo Stagg) to work 40 years as head coach at a single
   institution; 354 career wins rank him second all-time in
   Division I-A behind Bobby Bowden; portfolio includes two
   national championships (1982, 1986), five undefeated, untied
   teams, 21 Top 10 finishes, 21 bowl victories, five AFCA Coach
   of the Year plaques and more than 250 former players who
   played in the NFL (30 first-round picks); he's coached 70 first-
   team All-Americans and 24 first-team Academic All-Americans;
   chaired university fund-raising drives netting nearly $2 billion
   for Penn State; personally donated upwards of $4 million for
   scholarships, fellowships, professorships, interfaith spiritual
   center and library wing bearing his name.
THE GAME: Penn State versus Maryland, September 17, 1966

The Young Life of Joe Paterno

Joe Paterno was 23 years old and broke. It was 1950, and he had just completed his English literature degree at Brown University. He had designs on attending law school, which he'd been accepted into at Boston University, but he also carried financial debt ($2,000 worth of educational loans). He needed a job.

Rip Engle was 44 and moving up in the world. A former high school football coach, he'd taken the head coaching job at Brown in 1944 and compiled a 28-20-4 record in six seasons. Now he was moving to State College, Pennsylvania, as Penn State's new head coach. First, though, he called in a favor, asking Boston University coach Aldo "Buff" Donelli if he could spare an assistant's post at BU for Paterno, who'd quarterbacked Brown to an 8-1 season in 1949. Donelli said, "No problem."

Paterno never made it to Beantown. Before he could make the move, he heard from Engle. Penn State, forever loyal to its employees, was retaining its football assistants, men who had coached for years under Bob Higgins and then, in 1949, for Joe Bedenk. Engle was allowed to bring only one assistant with him from Brown. "He tried to get two other people to come with him," Paterno says, "but neither one wanted to leave and come to State College. At that time it was really in the wilderness."

Engle's third choice? Paterno. He was offered a $3,600 salary to serve as quarterbacks coach, and Paterno, just a few years older than most Nittany Lions players at the time, could live in a dorm with students to save dough. He took the deal, thanked Donelli anyway, and set out to save money, pay loans, and eventually return to Boston for law school.

"I was only going to do it for a year or two," Paterno says of coaching at Penn State, "and then I got the bug. I was young and all wrapped up in the football and the recruiting and the whole bit. So, you know, one year led to another, then after two or three years..."

Joe made the phone call.

* * *

Joe Paterno tasted victory in his first game as State's head coach, but after posting a 5-5 record in 1966, he holed himself up in his house, spent a summer overhauling his defense and laid the groundwork for a 30-0-1 run that would begin in the '67 season.

To understand Joseph Vincent Paterno, you must understand his father. Joe was the oldest of four kids born to Angelo and Florence Paterno. The Paternos raised Joe, his brother George, and his sister Cissy in the Flatbush section of Brooklyn. The two brothers played football together at Brooklyn Prep and later starred as the "Gold Dust Twins" at Brown, with George at running back and Joe at quarterback.

Angelo was self-made through and through. As a teen, he'd dropped out of high school to join General John J. Pershing's Army brigade in Texas. They'd been deployed by President Woodrow Wilson to protect the U.S.-Mexico border from the bandit attacks of Doroteo Arango, aka Francisco "Pancho" Villa, who sought revenge for America refusing to support his bid for the Mexican presidency.

Angelo later fought in World War I, then returned to the U.S. to complete his high school requirements. He earned a college degree attending night classes, and with a young family at home, he worked through law school at St. John's while serving as a State Supreme Court legal clerk. Angelo liked to read the newspaper with a dictionary next to him, and at the dinner table, arguing was not only allowed, it was encouraged. "You name it," Joe says, "we'd argue about it. Kids from the neighborhood would walk into our kitchen unannounced and just listen."

Joe was about 10 when Angelo, in his early 40s, passed the New York bar exam. Fifteen years later, his father's footsteps beckoning him back to Boston University Law, Joe made his infamous call home from State College. Florence picked up.

"Mom, I'm gonna be a coach," an excited Joe told her.

"What'd you go to college for?" she asked.

When Angelo got on the phone, he was more pained than confused. "My dad was a guy who loved the law," Joe says of Angelo, who, in 1955, died of a heart attack at age 58. "He was devastated. But to his credit, after a week or so, he called me back and said, 'If you're gonna be a coach, do a good job.'"

The Setting

Paterno once summed up his playing career at Brown by saying, "I wasn't really very good, but I was a hustler." Funny how themes recur. In 1950, with the Korean War in its infancy and 30,000-seat Beaver Field still on the west side of campus, Paterno moved into McKee Hall in West Halls. It was a short commute, close to the stadium, and across the street from the football offices in Rec Hall. Living in the dorms bred camaraderie between the young assistant and Penn State's players. "They used to play games on me, get me up in the middle of the night," Paterno says. "I was young, and I used to clown around with them and have a lot of fun. It had its ups and downs, but I enjoyed it." He pauses to draw a breath. "Some of the kids on that team have passed away, and some of their kids have played for me."

Penn State went 5-3-1 in 1950 and 5-4 the next year. Not bad, but not great for a program that had gone 9-0 in 1947 and tied Doak Walker's SMU team in the 1948 Cotton Bowl. The goal was to use football success to grow the school's national exposure. There was pressure to succeed, more pressure than Paterno or Engle had witnessed at an Ivy League institution like Brown.

Engle maintained an open-door policy for his assistants, and Paterno took advantage of it. After spending his first game as a coach—a 34-14 win against Georgetown on September 30, 1950—in the press box, Paterno apologized to Engle.

"I blew a couple of things, Coach," he said.

"Ah, you did all right," Engle replied reassuringly.

Another time Paterno came to Engle and stated, "Coach, I don't know how to coach."

"He said, 'Look, take some films,'" Paterno says. "In those days we had 16-millimeter films. 'Take some films and here's a projector. Chart everything you see. Come back and ask me if you have any questions.' So I spent three, four months—12, 14 hours a day—literally just looking at tapes."

Paterno's attention to detail and commitment for study accelerated his learning curve, as did that comfortable relationship with Engle and fellow assistants like Jim O'Hora, with whom Paterno shared a house for 11 years after leaving the dorms. Anything Paterno didn't understand—a blocking scheme, a play call, a new wrinkle in the offense—he could discuss with O'Hora. For his part, Engle included Paterno in his work whenever possible, like a late-night train ride the two once spent chatting football with Ohio State coach Woody Hayes. "Rip and Woody did the talking," Paterno says. "I did the listening."

The recruiting game came much more naturally to Paterno. He'd travel frequently, befriending coaches and impressing parents with his integrity. "You gotta believe in the program to begin with," he says. "I don't think you can fool kids. What I would do, I would try to get a feel for the place and I tried to outwork everybody. In those days, we didn't have as many restrictions as we have now. You never knew whether a kid was gonna show up or not in September, cause we didn't have a signing date. So it was a marathon.

"I believed in Rip and I believed in Penn State, and I went out and worked my butt off. If I got turned down—sometimes you learn more when you get turned down than when you get a kid—I would go back and analyze what I didn't do right and try to learn from that. Pretty soon you anticipate certain things, you know, if the coach is a little hostile to you, if he has associations with other universities, or if the family has certain issues. If you're a good salesman, you adjust."

By 1956, Paterno had made himself a coaching commodity. That year Weeb Ewbank, then coach of the NFL's Baltimore Colts, asked Paterno if he'd come on board as an assistant. Ewbank, who would lead the Colts to NFL championships in 1958 and '59 and the New York Jets to victory in Super Bowl III in 1968, had been Paterno's backfield coach and, for one year, his basketball coach at Brown. But Paterno opted to stay with Engle.

Paterno was later considered for the head-coaching gig at Boston College, but the one that cemented his future at Penn State was the Yale job. In 1963, a year after Paterno married wife Sue, Yale approached Paterno about its head-coaching vacancy before ultimately hiring John Pont. Two years later, after the '64 season, Pont left for Indiana, and Yale called Paterno to offer him the job.

Loyal to Engle, Paterno met with his friend and mentor. Both men agreed it was a good deal, but Paterno's preference was to stay in State College if the head job could someday be his. "That's the only reason I stayed," Paterno says. "I would have probably taken the Yale job if he hadn't indicated to me he was about ready to go."

Not long after the Nittany Lions beat Maryland 19-7 to complete a 5-5 1965 campaign, Engle called it a career. "The guy who was the athletic director, Ernie McCoy, the dean of the college of phys ed, called me into his office," Paterno says. "He said, 'Do you want the job?' I said, 'Yeah.' He said, 'Okay.' We shook hands and he said, 'You get 20,000 bucks a year.'"

It was February 19, 1966. The Joe Paterno Era had begun at Penn State.

The Game of My Life
By Joe Paterno

PENN STATE VERSUS MARYLAND
SEPTEMBER 17, 1966

As soon as I got the Penn State job, the first thing I did was run home and talk to my wife. We had a little place out here in one of the developments before we moved in where we are now. Then I went up in the office and I called every one of the recruits. I told everyone, "Look, I'm gonna be the head coach and I'm gonna give you a shot." In those days there was no letter of intent. So I told them that I felt good about the situation. And from there I went out and tried to see as many of them as I could. My memory might be playing games, but I don't think we lost anybody.

As we began preparing for that 1966 season, I tried to make sure I didn't pass up any details. As I recall now, I think I was a little bit too aggressive trying to prove to the guys that I could make decisions and things like that. You know, you go from where you're a colleague to where you're their boss, and I think in the process, I probably didn't listen enough. I probably didn't have enough confidence to sit back and say, "Okay, what are you guys thinking? Okay, I'll go along." Because I might have thought—and again, this is a long time ago—that I may have felt a little bit insecure. Or I didn't want to portray a lack of confidence.

So not just against Maryland, but that entire first year I probably was a little bit arbitrary, probably jumped at some things. Because I really didn't think I did a good job that year. In fact, the following year, I spent an awful lot of time trying to critique what I did. I spent a lot of time one-on-one with the assistant coaches, asking them to critique me after one year. That was probably the most productive part of my career, backing away and asking people what they thought after they had worked with me for a year.

As for 1966, well, you know, the year opened up with Maryland. Lou Saban had just taken the job there. Lou had won the AFL championship when he was up at Buffalo. Then he came to Maryland. I remember the whole atmosphere of the first game. ... I went out there, and I went through the little things that you say to the opposing head coach. I can't remember exactly what I said, except, "I'm glad you're back in college football, Lou." Cause Lou Saban had been a guy who was completely devoted to football.

At that time I called all the defenses, all the offensive plays; I ran the whole show, took over at halftime, the whole bit. When I was young, I was in everything. I was always a guy who was very active in the game, and felt I could help win the game. And that was one of my problems. I made some decisions along the way where somebody else on the staff probably could have done a better job.

The funny part about that Maryland game was, here I'm a young coach, it's my first game we're playing, and we're winning. I'm coaching against a guy who's a national figure. The guy's won championships. I knew we weren't very good, but I was just glad we had the best player on the field in Mike Reid. He was an unbelievable football player, one of the best that's ever played the game at defensive tackle.

So anyway, we win the game on three safeties by Mike Reid. He did it all. Then after the game, I'm running over to find Lou to do what you're supposed to do after a game. And I can't find him. He went right in! He calls me on Monday and says, "I apologize for not congratulating you, but we were both so lousy, I couldn't do it." I said, "Thanks, Lou." He was so upset. He had a lot of Pennsylvania kids on that team. He ended up firing about six or seven kids; he threw 'em right off the team.

Me, well, I thought we were great. We won! My first win. I thought, "Boy, what a great coach I am." Of course, the next game we played a great, great Michigan State team and lost 42-8. The one thing that sticks out from that game is my talk with [Spartans coach] Duffy Daugherty, who had been an assistant for Biggie Munn when they went undefeated in 1954 and '55. I walked off the field with him. He said, "Now look, listen to me. You're gonna be fine. Don't let this one distort you. When I first got to be the head coach at Michigan State, we lost five games. Everybody said I was a good assistant coach and I'd never be a good head coach."

He really gave me a pat on the back. I've never forgotten that. I've always appreciated it.

Game Results

Classes at Penn State had not started by September 17, 1966, so when the Maryland Terrapins arrived for the season opener, many of State's 21,000 students were not on hand. But 40,911 fans did show up on a warm, sunny day to soak up Paterno's first game as head coach.

Paterno then was much like Paterno now, telling the Associated Press before the game that there were at least four teams on the schedule—he named Michigan State, UCLA, Georgia Tech, and Syracuse—he didn't think Penn State could handle. Of course, by not mentioning Maryland, his comments became bulletin-board fodder for the Terps.

In 40 years as the Nittany Lions' head coach, Joe Paterno has celebrated 354 victories, including 21 bowl wins, more than any coach in college football history.

Early on, it looked like Maryland would capitalize on the perceived slight. After a penalty negated what would have been a 50-yard touchdown pass for Penn State, Maryland's Ernie Torgain scored from 15 yards out to make it 7-0 Terps. But unfortunately for Saban, that would be his club's high point of the afternoon.

In the second quarter, sophomore Mike Reid blocked a punt near Maryland's goalline. The Terps fell on the loose ball, but Reid was credited with a safety. 7-2. On the ensuing possession, Penn State drove 60 yards and scored on quarterback Jack White's 2-yard plunge. The score remained 8-7 when State's two-point conversion failed.

Tom Sherman tacked on a field goal before halftime to make it 11-7, and Reid & Co. had all the points they needed. Playing stingy defense, State held Maryland down in the third. Then, on the second play of the fourth quarter, Reid and defensive ends Bill Morgan and Bob Vukmer swarmed Maryland quarterback Al Pastrana for another safety, increasing the Lions' lead to 13-7.

Maryland's final scoring opportunity came midway through the fourth, when State fumbled near midfield and the Terps drove to the Lions' 8-yard line for a first-and-goal showdown. But on fourth down at the 1, Reid, with help from Jim Litterelle and John Runnells, came up with a clutch run stop to force a turnover on downs. Reid would add another safety, his third of the day, in the waning seconds to make it a 15-7 final in PSU's favor.

As that 1966 season progressed, Paterno's words proved prophetic, with Penn State losing to Michigan State, UCLA, Georgia Tech, and Syracuse. A 48-24 road rout of Pitt pushed State to 5-5 for the season, but Paterno was hardly satisfied.

"He spent the whole summer [of 1967] planning a new defense," wife Sue said years later. "Oh, that was rough, keeping the kids out of his hair and all. He said that if he didn't have a winning season the second year, he would quit and go back to assistant coaching. He said it wasn't fair to the kids to be coached by a loser."

Paterno clamped down on his program. In the years to come, his players would learn the meaning of hard work on the field and in class. "I've seen other coaches accept less than the best," said Bill Lenkaitis, who was a senior offensive lineman in 1967. "Joe never did that. He was a perfectionist. He'd keep us at practice forever."

The plain uniforms, the closely cropped hairdos, the little player notes he'd scribble to himself and cram into his pockets, the profanity box he instituted for kids who cussed or tossed a helmet—it all became part of the Paterno Way. "I don't want any hot dogs on my team," he once said. "If you're a hot dog, you tend to get careless in the clutch."

In 1973 Paterno rejected Boston Patriots owner Bill Sullivan's offer to become their coach and general manager for four years and $1.4 million. (He was earning $35,000 at the time from PSU.) Paterno remained loyal to State, and soon became known as just Joe or "JoePa" to the world of college football. Stories of him listening to Beethoven or Puccini while scripting game plans grew legendary. He was a professor of the game, a meticulous planner whose players in the 1970s took to calling him "The Rat" for his gravely, nasal intonation.

"Paterno has never forgotten," President Ronald Reagan once said, "that he is a teacher who's preparing his students not just for the season, but for life."

Reflecting on State

Much has changed at Penn State in the 40 years since Paterno replaced Engle as the 14th head coach in Penn State history. Everyone knows about the on-field success, the two national titles, the victories he's amassed, and generations of leaders he's influenced. But for all that's changed in State College, college football, and the world, Joe remains Joe, still living by the ethics and mantras that make him one of a kind.

Take the story he tells of the day his father walked in on him staring at a picture of himself in the *Brooklyn Eagle* newspaper. "You keep looking at it," Angelo told Joe. "Keep looking at it, you'll never see it in there again."

"My life has been dictated by, you'd better not look at the last picture, look at the next one," Paterno says. "I don't think anybody ever gets into something and thinks they're gonna stay in it as long as I've stayed where I am. I just thought, let me see if we can be better than we were in '66. And we were better in '67. One year leads to another. Before you know it, it's 20, 25, 30 years."

His approach has not changed much with age. He relies on his assistants more, the way he wishes he had as a rookie head coach. But he still does the recruiting waltz with moms and dads. He still gives as much of himself as he did when he pored over film of Engle's offense. He takes losses as hard as he did in the '60s, when he'd hole up in a room, inconsolable, after downers. He cried in a 2004 practice while thinking he could have done more to build a winning team that year for his outbound seniors. "Football keeps me alive," he once said.

Players have loved him. Others have butted heads with his policies. Many see the experience play out across the rest of their lives beginning with the day they leave his program. "The older I get," All-American tight end Ted Kwalik once said, "the smarter Joe Paterno gets."

"The longer you're away from Joe," Lenkaitis said, "the more you appreciate what he stands for. You realize it when you're trying to raise your own kids the right way. That's when you appreciate his values. I'm proud to be a Penn Stater because of Joe."

"He's a lot like your parents," former halfback Charlie Pittman once said. "It's sometimes difficult to appreciate them until you've grown and become a parent yourself."

And now, as he prepares to "leave meat on the bone" for the coach who will replace him, Paterno trudges on, refusing to leave a negative stamp on Penn State football. "Football got Penn State sports where they are today," says the youngest 80-year-old on the planet, fresh off the 2005 Big Ten championship and his first BCS bowl trip. "I think if we're gonna start to move ahead, I've got to get the football program back up where it belongs.

"I just hope I can be a good football coach. And when I get out of it, I hope I won't have screwed it up too much."

6

DENNIS ONKOTZ

NAME: Dennis Henry Onkotz
BORN: February 6, 1948, in Northampton, Pennsylvania
HOMETOWN: Northampton, Pennsylvania
CURRENT RESIDENCE: Boalsburg, Pennsylvania
OCCUPATION: Financial advisor, Pennsylvania Financial Group
POSITION: Linebacker
HEIGHT: 6 feet, 2 inches
PLAYING WEIGHT: 215 pounds
YEARS LETTERED: 1967 to 1969
NUMBER WORN AT PSU: 35
ACCOMPLISHMENTS: Three-year starter remains third all-time
    at Penn State in career tackles (287); 11 career interceptions
    are the most among any Nittany Lion linebacker; State's top
    punt returner from 1967 through 1969 ranks eighth in school
    history with a career 13.2-yard average; two-time first-team
    All-American was a third-round draft pick of the New York
    Jets in 1970; in 1995, he became then just the 12th Nittany
    Lion inducted into the College Football Hall of Fame.
THE GAME: Penn State at Syracuse, October 28, 1967

The Young Life of Dennis Onkotz

Dennis Onkotz was a perfect fit for the Joe Paterno system. He grew up in eastern Pennsylvania's working-class Cement Belt, came from a large family in a small town, loved sports, worked hard to improve as an athlete, excelled in school, and dodged trouble. He was a talented prep athlete and he knew it, but you wouldn't have caught him foretelling for himself a life of big-time college football and beyond. Humble yet motivated, Onkotz was just the way Paterno likes 'em.

"I didn't necessarily dream about college football, I just assumed I would go on and play somewhere," Onkotz says. "Maybe I had a big head, I don't know. Yeah, you dream about doing well and you fantasize a bit occasionally, but you're too busy playing the games, so you don't worry about those things. That's why I fit into Joe's philosophy: You take care of the little things, the big things take care of themselves."

Paterno couldn't have said it better himself. But it isn't a line coming from Onkotz. As a kid living in Northampton, his sports calendar constantly turned. He played sandlot baseball from the time he was old enough to round bases; he started organized football at six years old (the Konkrete Kids, his team's name, was a nod to limestone-rich Northampton's cement-producing roots); and he played basketball throughout high school. In the summer, Onkotz, second oldest of four kids, lifted weights with buddies, adding bulk to his thin, 6-foot, 2-inch frame.

Onkotz launched his football career as a guard—"Who wants to be a guard?" he says with a chuckle, adding, "I was never very good"—and played straight from first grade through seventh. In eighth grade he broke his collarbone and missed a season, a season he might have sat out anyway, having surpassed the league's weight limit.

His growth spurt continued. Onkotz didn't make the basketball team as a freshman at Northampton High, but by 10th grade, he'd grown six inches, cracked the hoops squad's starting five and blossomed into its leading scorer. He later became the school's first 1,000-point scorer.

Dennis Onkotz did it all in his Penn State career—covered the pass, stuffed the run, even returned punts. But his lone charge on October 28, 1967? Bottle up Syracuse's bruising back Larry Csonka.

Football progress took slightly longer. Onkotz hurt his right knee in a scrimmage before his junior year, and his coach, Al Erdosy, held him to defense only that season. He played safety wearing a knee brace. By then, though, he'd already impressed Penn State coach Rip Engle, who'd sent him a recruiting letter the previous year, in 1963. Onkotz never forgot it. In 1965, not long before Engle announced his retirement, Onkotz hitched a ride to State College with Erdosy in order to roam campus. The high school senior later returned with his parents for an official recruiting visit.

"Penn State, it was homey," says Onkotz, who also visited Syracuse, Army, Navy, Lehigh, and North Carolina. "I stayed with a player [John Kulka] in the dorm, where some other schools put you up at a hotel. What am I gonna do in a hotel at that age? I'm just a country boy.

"I felt very comfortable when I came for my visit. I grew up on the edge of a small town, and back in the '60s, State College was a small town. They had a place they took all the recruits called Home Delivery Pizza, and the owner … he made you feel comfortable."

The Setting

In the fall of 1966, Paterno was a new head coach trying to boost the national profile of the program he'd inherited six months earlier. Freshmen were ineligible that season, and at the time, they meant next to nothing to him. Little did Paterno know that his rookie class— Onkotz, Charlie Pittman, Don Abbey, Jim Kates, Neal Smith, Steve Smear, and others—would deliver Penn State success and recognition not previously enjoyed in the program's long history.

By the time Onkotz arrived for the start of October classes in 1966, the Lions had already played two games, defeating Maryland at home and stumbling miserably at Michigan State. He'd skipped the entire preseason, hanging back home to finish his summer job working with a crew at Bethlehem Steel. Once he joined his new crew of teammates, his job became taking bumps and bruises with the foreign team, learning how to adjust to college life before he absorbed PSU's playbook.

"Freshmen need time to acclimate, because you can easily get in trouble," Onkotz says. "Even then, I remember when midterms came, I realized I hadn't hardly studied. There were 10-week terms, and you know how fast that goes. That was my worst semester. I think I had a 2.2 [grade-point average] or something. That was a wakeup. You can just imagine if we had more football stuff going on."

Instead Paterno enforced mandatory study hall, and Onkotz began using the time for its intended purpose. He pulled up his grades while forging friendships with fellow freshmen George Kulka—younger brother of John, with whom Onkotz had bunked on his recruiting trip—Dave Rakiecki and Paul Johnson, Onkotz's first college roommate.

In the spring of 1967, Onkotz was groomed to play State's Hero position, a safety/linebacker charged with stuffing the run in Paterno's 4-4 scheme and then dropping back to cover tight ends or wideouts on passing downs. The youngster was suited for such a pivotal role, but he wasn't exactly pulled aside and promised a starting gig for the coming fall.

Instead, after a stellar spring, Onkotz went home to Northampton and his job at Bethlehem Steel, and when he returned for preseason practice, he found himself a second-stringer. On September 23, 1967, the Lions opened on the road at Navy, blowing a 22-17 lead with less than two minutes to play to fall, 23-22. "I think I played like two minutes," Onkotz recalls of the opener. "I knew I was better than…well, you know how that is. But yeah, I hardly played, and I'm thinking to myself, 'great coach we got here.'"

Onkotz was unaware that on the bus ride home from Annapolis, Maryland, Paterno decided to make a switch and play some new faces. Six days later, in humid 78-degree weather at the Orange Bowl in Miami, he did it. After starting the game with the same seniors who had allowed the winning score to Navy, Paterno began inserting sophomores one at a time. Smith. Kates. Onkotz and his buddy Rakiecki.

"I didn't know who was going in," Onkotz says of what turned into Penn State's 17-8 upset of the Hurricanes. "All of a sudden I was in the game, and I never came out. You have certain defenses, and we didn't have the right personnel in for those defenses, so I can remember just kind of filling in, not knowing what the heck I was doing at times. Like I had to become the middle guard at times, cause a middle guard wasn't in the game."

Onkotz rolled with it. He was where he felt he belonged—on the field in the middle of the action. Any potential awkwardness between him and the senior he replaced was erased when Paterno caught the senior after the game sneaking a beer at an airport bar and promptly threw him off the team.

"We don't want to mention names," Onkotz insists, "but I became the starting linebacker because he was gone. It was a get-your-attention type of thing. ... I was better than him. I don't think there's any doubt about that. But it's still tough to throw a senior off who's been starting for two years and move a young kid up."

Onkotz, 19 at the time, didn't disappoint. He started his first career game on October 7 against UCLA—a 17-15 Bruins victory—then, three weeks later, stood up to his toughest challenge yet: bruising back Larry Csonka and the Syracuse Orangemen.

The Game of My Life
By Dennis Onkotz

PENN STATE AT SYRACUSE
OCTOBER 28, 1967

Our defense was good that season. We shut people down. A lot of times, teams would score at the end of the game and it would kind of tick us off a little bit. You know, you hold people down to next to nothing and the subs go in—I don't like to say that—but you know, they score a touchdown or two.

We had speed. Everyone could run. That was the key. You had four actual linebackers, one was actually a defensive back, and you had the four linemen who were all running backs and linebackers in high school. So you had a whole team that could run. And with the 4-4, one linebacker was coming almost all the time, and you never knew which one. Once in a while we'd switch into the 5-3.

My strength was pass defense. In run defense, I may have been a little too small to be a middle linebacker. But I had speed. Dan Radakovich was my linebacker coach, so he helped with the mental part of the game. You have to think you're good and you have to react. If you're thinking while you're out there, you're beat. His philosophy was, if you do something wrong, do it full speed. You have a split second to make a decision and it has to be a reaction. I made some pretty good plays by making mistakes. But you make them full speed. You know you're not going to get chewed out, because everyone makes mistakes, but you make them full speed.

Syracuse was a big game back then for Penn State. Syracuse was the beast of the East. They were the team to beat. From a player's standpoint, I didn't have rivalries back then yet. But you could tell from the coaches that this was a big game. Syracuse coach Ben Schwartzwalder was still there.

The keys were different every game. The coaches used to read film and say, "This is the guy you watch," and your first step goes with him. After your first step you pick up another key. Well, you can imagine what my key was in that game: "Where Csonka goes, you go." That was key number one and key number two for me. Cause he was their offense.

We never trailed in that game, and it's always good to be ahead. I mean, if it's a close game, you're playing defense one way. If you're ahead or behind by a lot, it's a different game. So in that sense, it's the same as any other game. It doesn't really matter. Being ahead gives you an advantage, especially late in the game when you know they have to pass. You can hang back and pick one off.

As for Csonka, he was just a big, tough guy. The key to stopping him was getting him before he got up to full speed. And I was in on a lot of tackles that day. I remember being really sore after that game. I think I had 28 tackles in all, but you know, as you get older, maybe it'll be 32 next year, I don't know. I know there were a lot of contacts. I don't know how they do the stats, but I was beat up that game. My body hurt. That's the only game I remember being that beat up.

We had the lead in the fourth and they had to pass. I was in the under coverage, and you're supposed to throw over the linebacker, but

I got up and picked it off. Since I did a lot of running in high school, I was able to pick up my blockers and take it in. I remember throwing the ball up in the air after I scored. There was a picture in the paper where it said I threw the ball into the stands. I really didn't do that. I just threw it up in the air. I guess Joe never yelled at me for that, but in the future he would say, "Make believe you've been there before."

Game Results

No team ever really stopped Larry Csonka, Onkotz and the Lions included. The powerful fullback carried 32 times for 112 yards and two scores that afternoon in Syracuse's Archbold Stadium, and the Orangemen team captain went on to earn All-American honors that season, finishing his career with 2,934 rushing yards. Penn State, however, did win the battle of big plays, none bigger than Onkotz's fourth-quarter interception.

State, which had not beaten Syracuse since 1962 and had not won in Archbold since 1957, jumped out first on Charlie Pittman's 3-yard touchdown run. Csonka tied the game later in the first, but 15 seconds later, State quarterback Tom Sherman connected with All-American tight end Ted Kwalik for a 60-yard touchdown strike. 13-7 Lions.

Syracuse stuck with its game plan, dominating time of possession and offensive stats; the Orangemen collected 24 first downs and 363 total yards to PSU's 14 firsts and 283 yards. But the Lions never relinquished the lead. After a 22-14 margin was cut to 22-20, State senior tackle Mike McBath squelched one Syracuse drive by recovering a fumble. And later, with the Orange on the move again, Onkotz slipped in front of a Rick Cassata pass, leaped to snag it, then weaved 47 yards for a touchdown return, the first of three interception returns for touchdowns he'd have in his career.

The final was 29-20 Penn State, and the Nittany Lions were off and running, winning the last four games of the 1967 regular season, tying Florida State 17-17 in the Gator Bowl and not losing again until after Onkotz had played out his eligibility in the 1970 Orange Bowl.

Onkotz didn't bulk up much from his sophomore season, but as a junior and senior, he moved inside to play primarily against the run, relinquishing some coverage duties to fellow backer Jack Ham, a sophomore in 1968. Still, Onkotz never abandoned his versatile game, leading Penn State in tackles each of his three seasons (118 with 74 solos in 1967, 72 in '68, and 97 in '69)—an especially impressive stat considering he played alongside Lion greats like Ham, Kates, Smith, Smear, and Mike Reid. Onkotz also intercepted 11 balls in that span and regularly returned punts, including one for a touchdown as a senior.

As for that 29-0-1 streak he helped assemble? "Never thought about it," he says, "cause we were busy. We were full-time students. We all graduated in four years. There wasn't any time to think about it."

Reflecting on State

After his shaky start in the classroom, Onkotz graduated with a 3.5 GPA in biophysics and made Academic All-American in 1969. The following spring he was drafted by the New York Jets, who a year earlier had won Super Bowl III. Onkotz received a $15,000 signing bonus and $18,000 salary, but in just his ninth game with Gang Green, he broke two bones in his left leg, had pins inserted in the leg and spent the next five months in a cast.

"I think in today's world with rehabilitation and machines, I may have been able to come back," says Onkotz, who returned to Penn State for grad school while recuperating. "But I was on my own. You do a year and a half of essentially doing nothing, especially at that level, it's tough."

He didn't wallow. After earning a Master's degree in biophysics and working a few years for Corning Glass Works in State College, Onkotz turned down a transfer from Corning and jumped into financial work with help from a friend in the field. More than 30 years later, the father of four (all girls) and grandfather of two is still investing money for clients (ex-Nittany Lions among them), working in State College with the Pennsylvania Financial Group (Walnut Street Securities is his broker-dealer).

Onkotz caught up with several teammates at functions to celebrate his induction into the College Football Hall of Fame, but that's a decade in the past now, and he doesn't see many Class of '66ers anymore, despite living a healthy jog away from Beaver Stadium. If there's anything he does still see, it's the practicality of Paterno's teachings, like that age-old "take care of the little things" mantra. Or the priority list of life: "God, family, team," Onkotz says. "Just like Joe."

With the 40-year anniversary of his first college start approaching, Onkotz suspects fewer fans remember his team's accomplishments, but it doesn't faze him. He didn't play for glory then and he isn't bent on reliving anything now. That said, he won't deny the selflessness his recruiting class embodied, and how that translated to victories on Fridays and Saturdays.

"If you can do your job and count on the guy beside you to do his job, then you get good at what you're doing," he says. "Everyone did their job. Everyone was comfortable. And I think we liked each other. We got along. No one seemed to act like he was more important than anyone else."

That's football the Paterno Way.

7

CHARLIE PITTMAN

NAME: Charles Vernon Pittman
BORN: January 22, 1948, in Baltimore, Maryland
HOMETOWN: Baltimore, Maryland
CURRENT RESIDENCE: South Bend, Indiana
OCCUPATION: Senior vice president, Schurz Communications; former NFL player
POSITION: Halfback
HEIGHT: 6 feet, 1 inch
PLAYING WEIGHT: 190 pounds
YEARS LETTERED: 1967 to 1969
NUMBER WORN AT PSU: 24
ACCOMPLISHMENTS: Led Penn State in rushing and all-purpose yardage in 1967, '68 and '69; led Nittany Lions in scoring in '68 and '69; posted single-game career-high 177 yards against Navy in 1969; All-American and Academic All-American in 1969 was selected by St. Louis in third round of 1970 NFL draft; remains 10th in school history in scoring (192 points) and 12th in rushing (2,236 yards).
THE GAME: Penn State at Syracuse, October 18, 1969

The Young Life of Charlie Pittman

It isn't a line. When Charlie Pittman says his life never centered solely on sports, you know he's being straight. His focus growing up was on obtaining a balance between education and sports, and today his priorities haven't changed. As a teen, Pittman recognized football was a means to an education, a chance to avoid a lifetime working in a steel mill in his native Maryland. Thus, in 1966, after he was selected "Most Likely to Succeed" by members of his senior class at Baltimore's Edmondson High School, he wasn't about to squander his opportunity in the classroom.

"Some people might look at [the "Most Likely to Succeed" tag] in a trivial manner," says Pittman, a member of Joe Paterno's first recruiting class as Penn State's head coach. "But being selected ["Most Likely to Succeed"] is a burden. It's motivated me to continually want to succeed."

Pittman's road toward academic achievement began in West Baltimore, where he grew up passionate about reading and learning, much the influence of his mother, Jean. When school was out, Jean would call her four children into the house and ask them to read, then discuss their texts with her. It might be a novel, or maybe a newspaper or magazine. She wasn't picky.

Neighborhood kids laughed at the Pittmans when they'd eschew outdoor playtime for indoor book time. But no one was smirking when Charlie, son of a steelworker, stepped onto the gridiron in 1963 as a high school sophomore. Edmondson's program didn't have enough uniforms for every player, so Pittman needed to earn his jersey—literally. On the second day of practice, as a part of the team playing without team threads, he did just that. "They couldn't tackle me," Pittman says. "Coach [Augie Waibel] says, 'Get that guy a uniform!' I never gave it up."

After playing jayvee as a sophomore, Pittman's Edmondson teams didn't lose a game his junior and senior seasons. Recruiters circled: Ohio State, Notre Dame, Maryland, Penn State. Pittman narrowed his options to Penn State and Maryland. Penn State coach Rip Engle had dispatched his backfield coach, George Welsh, to recruit Pittman, and

Charlie Pittman (#24), both an All-American and Academic All-American as a senior in 1969, never lost a game after he joined the first-team offense in 1967. He completed his career with Penn State riding a 31-game unbeaten streak.

Welsh had locked up a verbal commitment from the running back. Then, after the 1965 season, Engle announced his retirement. Paterno was named his successor.

"Rip called me to tell me he was retiring," Pittman says. "I said, 'If I'm coming to Penn State, I'm coming to play for Rip Engle.' Joe Paterno? I don't know anything about Joe Paterno. So I told Rip, 'No, I'm not coming.' I called Lou Saban at Maryland and told him I was ready to sign with him.

"Then Rip called me back with Paterno on the phone. Rip assured me Paterno was going to be a good football coach and things weren't going to change. They tried to convince me."

Pittman slept on it. After volleying it in his mind, he phoned Saban. "Saban said, 'We can guarantee you can start as a sophomore. If you go to Penn State, do you honestly think you're good enough to start as a sophomore?'" Pittman recalls. "Why did he say that? He questioned my ability and challenged me at the same time. I said to myself, 'I'll show you. I'm coming to Penn State.'"

The Setting

Things weren't easy for Pittman when he arrived in University Park for fall semester 1966. While President Lyndon B. Johnson faced growing criticism against war in Vietnam, Pittman soon was fighting his own inner conflict over whether to remain at Penn State.

Though he was regularly called on as a scout team member to impersonate top backs of Penn State's opponents—he doubled as Mel Farr (UCLA), Clint Jones (Michigan State), and Floyd Little (Syracuse)—Pittman remained stuck as a third-stringer on State's freshman team. He'd break off a sweet rumble in practice only to receive lukewarm feedback from freshman coach Earl Bruce. One day that fall, Charlie called home. "I told my mother, 'Bruce is picking on me. I don't need this. I'm coming home,'" Pittman says. "Then my father [Charlie Sr.] gets on the phone and tells me, 'If you leave there, you can't come home. If other people are doing it, you can do it. You don't want to work in a steel mill. Stay there and gut it out.'"

The freshman team played two games that semester. After one contest in which Pittman only carried the ball twice, he recalls dragging his way to practice, head glued to his chest. He passed Paterno, who was walking with a man Pittman later learned was an NFL scout.

"Hey Charlie, how'd you do in the game?" Paterno asked.

"I only got to carry the ball two times for 14 yards," responded the dejected freshman.

"Well, the next time somebody asks you," Paterno said, "tell him you averaged seven yards a carry."

Pittman smiled. He turned around, and while still within earshot, he heard Paterno tell the scout, "That's the guy who's gonna make me a great football coach someday."

Pittman felt immediate inspiration. "No more calls home," he says.

In the spring of 1967, Pittman aimed to prove he was the best back on campus, which meant keeping up with Bobby Campbell, who had led the 1966 team in rushing. Campbell was the established back, but Pittman was hungry.

Campbell started the season as first string, but he went down with an injury in Penn State's third game, a 17-15 loss to eventual '67 Heisman winner Gary Beban and UCLA. Paterno called on Pittman. He started for the first time the next week, joining a host of fellow sophomores—Pete Johnson, Neal Smith, Steve Smear, Jim Kates, and Dennis Onkotz—who'd begun playing regularly since the Miami tilt two games earlier.

Pittman didn't disappoint. First Penn State thumped Boston College 50-28. Then, after Paterno nudged him to run with one hand on the ball versus two, the young halfback returned a kickoff 83 yards for a score and finished with 265 all-purpose yards—still a Penn State sophomore record—in a 21-14 Homecoming win against West Virginia.

Soon after, Campbell returned to practice.

Recalls Pittman: "Joe says, 'All right, Blue in the huddle.' Blue means first team. Both Campbell and I went to the huddle at the same time. So I'm standing there and he's standing there. I couldn't tell him to get out of the huddle and he wasn't going to tell me to get out of the huddle. Then Joe says, 'Campbell, get out. You gotta earn your spot back.' Ohhhhh. What a vote of confidence for me."

Pittman kept his starting spot, and the Nittany Lions kept winning. Seven straight in 1967, blemished only by a 17-17 tie with Florida State in the Gator Bowl. The following season, Paterno's offensive philosophy remained simple: Run the ball, own the clock, let the defense do its thing. With Mike Reid and Smear in the middle and a Linebacker U class paced by Jack Ham, Onkotz, and Kates, the

Lions rolled to a 10-0 regular season, holding opponents to 13 or fewer points in eight of those games. A come-from-behind, 15-14 win against John Riggins-led Kansas in the Orange Bowl sealed the perfect season.

Pittman credits some of his own success at that time to practicing against such a ferocious defense. Tuesdays of game weeks—or Bloody Tuesdays, as they were called—were the worst: backs versus backers, one-on-one blocking drills. Linebackers coach Dan "Bad Rad" Radakovich roamed the locker room those days, whispering promises of pain to running backs. "My linebackers are gonna get you guys today," Radakovich would purr, grinning devilishly. "We're just waiting for you." Backs coach George Welsh could only protect his players so much. "You'd get a beating," Pittman says. "They weren't happy 'til they drew blood. By senior year, I was always hurt on Tuesdays just to avoid those drills."

Come Penn State's 1969 clash against Syracuse at aging, cranky Archbold Stadium, the Nittany Lions' unbeaten streak stood at 23. Two of those wins had been against Syracuse: a 30-12 whipping at home in 1968 and a hard-earned 29-20 triumph against Larry Csonka's Orangemen at Archbold in 1967. Before '67, the 'Cuse had won seven of the previous nine meetings. Clearly, momentum had now shifted back in Penn State's favor.

The Lions still possessed a stingy, swarming defense, and they had added backfield pop in sophomores Lydell Mitchell and Franco Harris. Rushing behind an offensive line of Tom Jackson, Bob Holuba, Warren Koegel, Charlie Zapiec, and Vic Surma, the backs—Pittman, Mitchell, and Harris—were nearly unstoppable. The three split carries, confounded opposing defenses, and gobbled yardage. If one didn't burn you, another would. That had proved clutch when Pittman sprained an ankle earlier in the season against Colorado, leaving the youngsters to emerge against the Buffs and Kansas State. Harris had scored in State's 27-3 win against Colorado, and Mitchell carried 19 times for 123 yards in a 17-14 defeat of Kansas State. Syracuse was facing a three-headed monster.

The Game of My Life
By Charlie Pittman

PENN STATE AT SYRACUSE
OCTOBER 18, 1969

As a kid I'd wanted to go to Syracuse to wear Jim Brown's number 44. In those days, if you were a running back, they attracted you to Syracuse by offering you that number. But Syracuse never recruited me, so I always wanted to play well against them.

In 1969, Syracuse coach Ben Schwartzwalder really wanted to beat Penn State. He didn't like what had happened the year before. And early on, I'm telling you, we were not playing well. They stopped us on everything we could possibly do. Our defense was doing okay, but offensively we were just three and out, three and out.

Our defensive players were getting mad. They were saying, "When are you guys gonna do something?" Al Newton scored twice for Syracuse to make it 14-0, and that was a lot of points on our defense. They were saying they were tired because we left them on the field too long. We just didn't get any drives.

At halftime it was 14-0 and Joe was livid. Oh, was he hot. In the locker room, he made all his adjustments and corrections. Then, right when it was time to go out, he stopped us and said, "You guys are stinking up the place. You're just playing lousy." Then he said, "Now I want you to go out there, and whatever you do, don't embarrass me, don't embarrass this university, don't embarrass your parents, don't embarrass your team and don't embarrass yourself. Because that's the way you're playing. You're playing to embarrass everybody. Now get out there and play!"

I'd never seen him like that before. Don't embarrass your family? Now that rung a bell. Still, it didn't happen right away. In fact, we played three lousy quarters. But we always said we own the fourth quarter. That was our motto: fourth quarter's ours. I got the offense together and said, "All right, Lydell, Franco, we gotta do this!" They said, "I'm with you. Let's find a way to do it."

We got a big run out of Franco on a draw play. We started moving the ball. Then there was a long pass play down the left sideline, and pass interference was called on the guy covering me, and we got the ball inside the 5. Schwartzwalder was livid. He came on the field and was screaming at the officials. But it was definitely pass interference. He was on my back.

After Lydell scored our first touchdown, Joe decided to go for two. I had no idea what he was thinking, but he was smart enough to think ahead. He knew he wasn't going to play for the tie, so he was going to have to go for two one of the times. He figured the defense wasn't going to let them score any more points.

When they called holding on our first try for two, Schwartzwalder got hot again. That was the second big call to go against him. I remember afterwards he said, "The officials took the game. They were intimidated by Paterno."

On the other side, I think when you get a call like that, you get motivated. You get fired up and say, "Hey, maybe things are turning in our favor." Franco scored the two points on the next attempt, and he scored again later in the quarter to give us the lead. After that, I remember us getting together and saying, "Told you we could do this!"

The thought of losing never entered our minds that day. We knew we'd played lousy, but we just hadn't fired our best shots yet. When you have a win streak like that, you don't think, oh, the streak's gonna end. You think, we're gonna find a way to win this. When are we gonna make the play to pull it out? That game probably helped us win the Orange Bowl that season cause we'd been there before. We'd played a tough game.

Game Results

The defense gave up two first-half scores, but it also kept State in the game. In front of 42,291 fans on a gray day in the concrete canyon of Archbold, State's George Landis blocked two George Januszkiewicz first-half field goal attempts. Late in the half, those blocks in mind, Schwartzwalder went for it on fourth down inside State's 5. But Tony

Allen was stuffed on a sweep. "If they score," Paterno said of that play, "it's all over. That was the turning point."

Still down 14-0 in the fourth quarter to the unranked Orange, Penn State's Jack Ham recovered a fumble on Syracuse's 32. Following a controversial pass interference play involving Pittman and 'Cuse linebacker Richard Kokosky, Mitchell punched it in from 4 yards out to get the Nittany Lions on the board. Paterno went for two, and Harris was stacked up on a swing pass, but a holding call gave Penn State a second chance. With Schwartzwalder barking from the home sideline and boos raining down on the officials, Harris scampered around left end to cut it to 14-8 Orangemen.

Later in the fourth, Ham deflected a Syracuse punt, setting up the Lions on the Orange 36. Two plays later, quarterback Chuck Burkhart faked to Pittman off tackle, handing instead to Harris, who split the defense and rumbled 34 yards to knot the game, a tie that was broken seconds later by kicker Mike Reitz's extra point. "We were down and looking at our first loss of the year," Ham says, "and we ended up winning on a day when, by all rights, we should have lost."

"It was a tough one for us," Mitchell said, "but those are the types of games you have to win sometimes. They're not all gonna be pretty. They're not all gonna be easy. Those are the ones when you come together as a team."

Penn State extended its unbeaten streak to 24 games, but Schwartzwalder wasn't finished. Two days later the Syracuse coach told a group gathered at the New York Football Writers luncheon that officiating had cost his team the game. He complained to the Eastern College Athletic Conference, saying "Pennsylvania officials" flagged Syracuse while overlooking Penn State penalties.

Meanwhile, Pittman and the Lions were emboldened by the dramatic victory. They mauled Ohio 42-3 the next week at home. Then, on November 1, Pittman, Harris, and Mitchell ran for more than 100 yards apiece as Penn State beat Boston College 38-16.

With the streak alive at 29-0-1, No. 3-ranked Penn State accepted an early bid to the Orange Bowl. Michigan upset No. 1 Ohio State, but by then it was too late for Penn State to back out of its Orange Bowl commitment and play new No. 1 Texas in the Cotton Bowl in what would have been a true national championship game.

After Texas' regular-season finale win against Arkansas, President Richard Nixon presented the Longhorns with a plaque pronouncing them the nation's No. 1 team, telling the Horns, "I want you to enjoy this because it has cost me a lot of votes in Pennsylvania." Despite Penn State's gutsy Orange Bowl win against a high-powered Missouri team—the Lions picked off Tigers QB Terry McMillan seven times in the 10-3 victory—Texas' defeat of Notre Dame in the Cotton Bowl denied Paterno his first national championship. "If we would have played," State linebacker Dennis Onkotz said, "I think there would have been a new No. 2."

Reflecting on State

Having never lost as a starter in three years of college ball, Pittman left Happy Valley for an NFL career. Taken in the third round of the 1970 draft, he became primarily a kick returner, playing one year with the St. Louis Cardinals followed by one season with the Baltimore Colts. In 1972 he was planning a move to the Canadian Football League when he crossed paths with Paterno at a banquet.

"Charlie, what are you doing with your career?" the coach asked.

"Well, I wasn't doing well in the NFL, so I'm going to Canada to give it one more shot," Pittman responded.

"Charlie," said Paterno, placing a hand on his former All-American's shoulder, "you don't need to do that. I get the feeling you're trying to prove to people that your college career was not a fluke. You don't owe that to anyone. Think about it and call me next week. I know there's a gentleman in Erie [Pennsylvania] who would love to have you work for him."

Pittman discussed it with his family, and he realized his coach was right. His heart wasn't it. He called Paterno's contact, landed a banking job in Erie, and stayed there for seven years. Then he broke into the newspaper business, working first for the Mead family in Erie and then Knight Ridder, with which he later nearly became publisher of the *Centre Daily Times*.

Today, Pittman manages 10 daily newspapers, three weeklies, and a shopper for Schurz Communications. The father of three—two of his kids went to Penn State, including son Tony, a defensive back with the undefeated 1994 team that won the Rose Bowl—still finds time for phone chats with old friends like Mitchell and Harris. Plus he returns to his alma mater once each fall, back to the place where a 30-0-1 run remains forever frozen in time.

"I haven't scored a touchdown in 35 years, and people still remember," Pittman says. "I played with some great football players, and we learned a lot from each other. It was a real growing-up experience. And it changed my life for the better."

8

LYDELL MITCHELL

NAME: Lydell Douglas Mitchell
BORN: May 30, 1949, in Salem, New Jersey
HOMETOWN: Salem, New Jersey
CURRENT RESIDENCE: Baltimore, Maryland
OCCUPATION: National sales manager for Super Bakery Inc.;
former NFL player
POSITION: Halfback
HEIGHT: 6 feet
PLAYING WEIGHT: 198 pounds
YEARS LETTERED: 1969 to 1971
NUMBER WORN AT PSU: 23
ACCOMPLISHMENTS: Led Penn State in rushing in 1970 and
'71; finished career with 2,934 rushing yards (sixth in school
history), 15 100-yard games (including two 200-yarders) and
38 rushing touchdowns (tops in PSU history); scored five
times in a game twice in '71 to finish with 29 TDs (26
rushing) for 174 points, the best single-season scoring total in
school history; 1971 consensus All-American played nine pro
seasons with Baltimore, San Diego and Los Angeles, making
three Pro Bowls. In 2004, he became the 19th member of
Penn State's program inducted into the College Football Hall
of Fame.
THE GAME: The Orange Bowl, Penn State versus Missouri,
January 1, 1970

The Young Life of Lydell Mitchell

The Rams of Salem High form a line outside the locker-room door, their crisp blue-and-white uniforms and glossy helmets glistening in the light. It's a quarter-mile walk to the stadium, the place to be on a fall Friday night in this southwestern New Jersey town. They begin to march two and three abreast, their mission clear, their adrenaline maxed, their eyes fixed straight ahead.

This is—was—Lydell Mitchell's boyhood. He still pictures it with youthful lucidity. He remembers himself as a wide-eyed, speechless kid bouncing alongside the rows of Rams as they clicked and clacked their way to home turf. He was a fan in awe of his idols. Years later, that kid wore the same glorious threads while inspiring waves of future Rams.

"That was part of the fabric of the city, wanting to be a Salem Ram," Mitchell says. "Wearing that blue and white was something to look forward to."

The second of three children, Mitchell possessed natural athleticism, which he never hesitated to brandish on the baseball diamond, basketball court, or even a makeshift soccer pitch. But the son of two factory workers owned an extra intangible. He was good and he knew it.

Such confidence, even cockiness, meshed with a desire to work more diligently and sweat more profusely than his competitors, spawned a tireless athlete. He played four years each of varsity football, basketball, and baseball. We're talking no freshman ball, no jayvee. He became a Salem star as a ninth-grader.

Mitchell's first recruiting letter arrived during that freshman year. Its author? Penn State football coach Rip Engle. Fierce jockeying followed for the running back/defensive back's services: Michigan, Notre Dame, and Ohio State were but a few of the many schools to recruit him. In 1967, Penn State trailed Maryland (Mitchell's girlfriend at the time was planning to attend school in College Park, Maryland) and Ohio State (his grandparents lived in Columbus, Ohio) in the Mitchell sweepstakes.

He settled on becoming a Buckeye, but before committing to Woody Hayes at Ohio State, Mitchell fielded one final in-home visit

Lydell Mitchell wasn't originally happy about his role in Penn State's offensive game plan for the 1970 Orange Bowl. But in the end, his catch and run for a touchdown marked the only points scored by either team in the Nittany Lions' defeat of Missouri.

from Joe Paterno, who'd succeeded Engle at Penn State in 1966. The coach was blunt. Paterno told Mitchell he was only passing on Penn State because he thought he'd never play with Charlie Pittman entrenched at running back. "He challenged me," Mitchell says, "and I told him I was coming to Penn State, and I was gonna break Charlie's records. I guess he knew what buttons to push to motivate me. Had he not come in, I would have gone to Ohio State."

The Setting

It didn't take long to see why Paterno had visited Mitchell's living room. In 1969, Mitchell and fellow sophomore Franco Harris joined Pittman to form one of the nation's most formidable backfield trios. Paterno preferred using Mitchell as a wing back, catching passes out of the backfield as often as he took a handoff from quarterback Chuck Burkhart. But when Pittman, a preseason All-American, sprained an ankle in the season's home-opening win against Colorado, Mitchell was pressed into tailback duty.

The next week, his first career start, Mitchell bailed out No. 2-ranked State in a nip-and-tuck affair at No. 20 Kansas State. Late in the first half, he flashed breakaway speed on a 58-yard touchdown romp for the game's first points. He showed durability by sustaining the Nittany Lions' offense that day, carrying the ball 19 times for 123 yards in a 17-14 win. Though the close margin of victory dropped State to No. 5 in the polls, there was no looking back for Paterno's running back of the future.

"Joe just said, 'Hey, I can't hold them back any longer,'" Mitchell says of himself and good friend Harris. "I'm saying to myself, 'What took you so long?' You know? This is gonna happen. You can't please everybody, and I think that's what he tried to do sometimes, appease guys."

In Pittman, Mitchell had a guidance counselor and a bar of excellence to strive for. Penn State hadn't lost a game since Pittman joined the starting offense early in the 1967 season. But now, despite their bond as teammates—a bond strengthened by being African-Americans when most of campus, and most of the roster, was white—

Mitchell wanted Pittman's job. "It's not that you don't pull for the other guy," Mitchell says. "But at the same time, you watch him and say, 'Man, I want to be better than him.' It's kind of a friendly contest."

In the fall of 1969, pundits who still doubted Penn State's place among traditional powers were silenced as Mitchell & Co. carried the Nittany Lions to a second straight undefeated season. While the Lions' win streak crept along, Mitchell grappled with his role. He was good enough to be the feature back at most schools in America, yet here he was splitting carries as his first year of eligibility dwindled. Pittman's ankle injury had allowed Mitchell to become Penn State's leading rusher by the time State traveled to play Pitt in the second-to-last game of the season. But then the sophomore hardly touched the ball in a 27-7 win against the archrival Panthers. And when the regular season ended a week later with a win against N.C. State, Mitchell (616 yards on 113 carries) found himself third on the team in rushing yards behind Pittman (706) and Harris (643).

"Everybody likes to be the leading rusher, and I ended up going from first to third, so it bothered me," Mitchell says. "But that's good that it bothered me. Because if I was complacent and said, 'I'm okay with this,' then I certainly wouldn't have had the drive that I had. So I was ticked off about it. It took me a while to get over it."

In fact, Mitchell was still stewing in December 1969 as Penn State prepared for Missouri in the Orange Bowl on New Year's Day.

The Game of My Life
By Lydell Mitchell

THE ORANGE BOWL
PENN STATE VERSUS MISSOURI
JANUARY 1, 1970

In 1969 I learned that defenses win football games. And our defense was just fantastic. I mean, they were so good, it was unreal. We didn't have to do much offensively, just get out of our own way. So our game plan for Missouri was very simple: just run. That's all we ever did. I mean Chuck Burkhart was a great guy and everything, but as far as throwing the football, he wasn't that talented, just very efficient.

When I got to Florida (for the Orange Bowl), I found out I only had one running play. It was a scissors play where I would flank out like an inside reverse, but I would flank outside the tight end, come back underneath over center, and they'd give me the ball. That was the only play I had. I was really mad.

Joe had also put in this pass play for me, but I wouldn't run it. I mean, I was so mad that when they'd call the play in practice, I'd just jog out there. I was so distraught, I'd just run out there and turn around. The timing was never right. Till this one instance, when I turned around, and Joe was right behind me. He says to me, "You know what? You're gonna be a pretty good player one day." I said, "Man, you gave me one play to run." Just like that. He said, "I put this pass play in for you, so I would suggest that you practice it, because you're gonna score a touchdown on it." I went on and on about the one play that he gave me, but eventually I came to my senses and started practicing the pass play. Sure enough, that was the winning touchdown.

It happened late in the first quarter. The play was like those I'd later run in professional football. It was an option play where I could go inside or outside. I had to read the defense. I caught the pass and made one of my greatest moves. It was against Roger Wehrli, who played for Missouri and went on to become an All-Pro for the St. Louis Cardinals. My feet were so fast; it was unreal when I made the move. I was shuffling and made him miss me. It was beautiful. He looked like he was straight out parallel. He just dove for me, and I made him miss and scored on it. It made Joe look like a genius. The guy put this play in purposely for me—at least that's what he told me—and it worked.

The rest of the way was all defense. It was just up and down, two titans fighting out there. I remember one play I made where I saved a touchdown on a punt return. In those days, we stayed in for the punt. Jon Staggers was going to score, but I caught him and saved the touchdown. Then our defense held 'em. I remember Mike Reid saying if we had to hold 'em, we would have held 'em all day.

After the game, I don't think I paid any attention to Joe. It was self-gratification that I had gone out there and scored the touchdown. I was into myself. I didn't care what he was saying. I'd done my thing. It was also gratifying to keep the streak alive, but obviously the seniors were the guys who got the credit. They had played a significant part in it. Though we had a lot to do with it, it was their moment.

Sure, it was disappointing not to be No. 1 after that, but I didn't understand the magnitude of the game at the time. Besides, I was more consumed with the play-calling. I've never forgotten it. But it was a learning experience for me. That game helped me mature. I think that's where I really grew up.

Joe used to always tell us, "Take care of your knitting"—take care of your business. If I didn't take care of my business, things wouldn't work out. So that's what it was about, and that particular game was a significant turn in my life. It just got better from there.

Game Results

Mitchell's touchdown was the lone blip of offensive fun in an otherwise defense-shrouded Orange Bowl. That was surprising considering the 9-1 Tigers had averaged 36 points and 450 yards of offense per game coming in. Missouri was balanced, and Paterno knew it, calling it "the first really modern offensive college football team." Terry McMillan was a deft passer, running back Joe Moore had topped 1,300 yards on the ground that year, and Mel Gray had caught 26 passes for 705 yards.

Penn State did all of its scoring in the first quarter. Before a roaring crowd of 77,282, Mike Reitz capped a drive deep into Mizzou territory by nailing a 29-yard field goal to make it 3-0 with 3:44 left in the first. On the ensuing kickoff, Reid drilled Moore, jarring the ball loose. Penn State recovered the fumble at Missouri's 28. On the next play, Burkhart hit Mitchell on the left sideline. The sophomore juked Wehrli, picked up a block, and blazed in for six points. In a 21-second span of game clock, State had jumped out to a 10-0 lead.

Penn State's renowned bend-but-don't-break defense was at its best. On Missouri's four possessions after Mitchell's touchdown, the

Tigers imploded four times inside Penn State territory on three McMillan interceptions and a fumble recovery by John Ebersole. Late in the half, Missouri reached the Lions' 7-yard line, but Reid dropped Moore for a 10-yard loss, and an incompletion later, Missouri settled for a field goal to make it 10-3.

The teams traded jabs and turnovers in the second half. Penn State could have iced matters in the fourth, but Reitz blew what should have been an easy field goal attempt, and the nail-biting continued. Then, late in the fourth, with Chuck Roper in for an injured McMillan at quarterback, Missouri drove from its 42 to State's 14 with 1:42 left. After two incompletions, State's George Landis clinched the 10-3 victory by picking off a pass at the 2 and returning it nearly to midfield.

The final tally was staggering. Led by All-Americans Reid, Dennis Onkotz, and Neal Smith, Penn State intercepted seven passes, recovered two fumbles, and held the Tigers to six completions for the game. The Lions may have finished a controversial second in the polls behind undefeated Texas, but its defense was unmatched: In 11 wins, State pitched two shutouts, held two teams to three points each, one to seven, and another to eight. Eleven games, 90 points allowed.

Reflecting on State

Mitchell witnessed a little of everything at Penn State. He played a key role as a sophomore with that remarkable '69 team; he saw the school-record 31-game win streak snapped at Colorado as a junior in 1970; and he starred in a 30-6 thumping of Texas in the 1972 Cotton Bowl. Mitchell gained 146 yards on 27 rushes against the Longhorns—he's since been elected to the Cotton Bowl Hall of Fame—and found similar success in the NFL.

In 1972, Mitchell graduated from Penn State with a degree in secondary education and was drafted in the second round by the Baltimore Colts. The New Jersey native topped 1,000 yards rushing three times in his nine NFL seasons and thrice led the league in receiving. He retired in 1980, and despite an interest in attending law school—to this day he regrets never pursuing a law degree—Mitchell went into business with Harris selling natural fruit bars on a stick.

He never left the food business. He and Harris ran the Parks Sausage company for years (they've since sold off the company's manufacturing plant) and today they operate Super Bakery, a name inspired by Harris' four Super Bowl trips with the Pittsburgh Steelers. Mitchell travels frequently in a bid to "revolutionize the doughnut market" by selling a healthier doughnut with less fat, less sugar, and 14 vitamins and minerals. Schools are his top clients.

"I have a passion for selling," he says, "going out every day and trying to improve our company, telling our story, trying to get better day in and day out with the same work ethic I had playing football."

Speaking of football, it's never far from Mitchell's mind. Induction into the College Football Hall of Fame in 2004 had him reflecting on his college years. "Millions of players have played the game," he says, "but how many are in the Hall of Fame? 800? Absolutely incredible. This is truly a dream come true."

Of course, it would have been nice had his 1970 Orange Bowl heroics helped the Nittany Lions win their first national title. "But," he says, "everything's done in time. There are always steps. This group built it to this level, another group built it to another level. We certified that Penn State's a powerhouse. And the guys after us continued the tradition."

9

JOHN CAPPELLETTI

NAME: John Raymond Cappelletti
BORN: August 9, 1952, in South Philadelphia, Pennsylvania
HOMETOWN: Upper Darby, Pennsylvania
CURRENT RESIDENCE: Laguna Niguel, California
OCCUPATION: Partner in Rancho Santa Margarita, California-based AlphaBio, Inc.; former NFL player
POSITION: Running back
HEIGHT: 6 feet, 1 inch
PLAYING WEIGHT: 215 pounds
YEARS LETTERED: 1971 to 1973
NUMBER WORN AT PSU: 22
ACCOMPLISHMENTS: Led Penn State in rushing in 1972 and '73; A consensus All-American in 1973, he rushed for 1,522 yards and 17 touchdowns that season; '73 campaign included three consecutive 200-yard games, then an NCAA record; won Heisman Trophy, Maxwell Award and Walter Camp Player of the Year in '73; remains lone Heisman winner in school history; played nine NFL seasons with Los Angeles Rams and San Diego Chargers; inducted into College Football Hall of Fame in 1993.
THE GAME: Penn State versus N.C. State, November 10, 1973

The Young Life of
John Cappelletti

In the beginning, he wasn't John Cappelletti, Heisman winner and Penn State legend. There were no moving speeches to improvise, no movies to inspire, no NFL careers to launch. He was just John, and he was like a lot of kids. He loved his family—dad John Sr., an Italian immigrant, mom Anne, older brother Martin and younger siblings Michael, Jeannine, and Joey—and he spent much of his free time transfixed on sports.

In the 1960s, the Cappellettis lived in Upper Darby, Pennsylvania, west of Philadelphia's city limits. They had relatives throughout eastern Pennsylvania and southern New Jersey, so the family's weekends were dotted with christenings, weddings, and other get-togethers.

John, two years younger than Martin, played Little League baseball with his older brother and continued with the sport up through American Legion. For inspiration, John became a diehard Phillies fan. In the winters he switched to the NHL's Flyers for rooting purposes and to Catholic Youth Organization hoops teams for his own athletic pursuits. Falls, well, falls were special. From a young age, when he'd followed another Italian athlete with his same surname—wide receiver/kicker Gino Cappelletti (no relation) of the Boston Patriots—he'd nurtured a dream to one day "go pro" himself.

College, of course, would come first, and there was much to learn. Take the Heisman Trophy, for example. John hadn't even heard of the Heisman name until younger brother Michael began attending Malvern Prep on scholarship from a benefactor named Alan Ameche, Wisconsin's 1954 Heisman winner. Michael once saw the actual trophy at the Ameches' house and told John about it. (Michael later wed Ameche's daughter, Catherine.)

John's high school team, Monsignor Bonner, in nearby Drexel Hill, Pennsylvania, played its home games in Villanova's stadium, so the Wildcats were one of the programs Cappelletti was strongly considering when his senior year began in 1969. He was also pondering Miami (Florida), Penn State, Ohio State, and Virginia

John Cappelletti was a workhorse in 1973, rushing for 1,522 yards, nearly half of which came in a three-game run of consecutive 200-yard games. Perhaps none of those performances was gutsier than the Heisman winner's 41-carry, three-touchdown day against N.C. State.

Polytechnic Institute (now Virginia Tech), the last of which Cappelletti visited at the request of then coach Jerry Claiborne. As he did for many Penn State running backs of the era, PSU assistant George Welsh recruited Cappelletti, eventually giving way to head coach Joe Paterno for the final hard sell in the Cappellettis' living room.

But John's decision to attend State was determined by more than Paterno's charming influence on John Sr. and Anne. It was John's youngest brother Joey's struggle with leukemia that led John to University Park. "Having a brother that was sick, my parents certainly weren't going to get on a plane and fly to Miami or even Ohio State," John says. "At that point, I had to narrow it down to a school within driving distance. And even that later became a chore for them at times."

Not that the Cappellettis ever let on. From the day their second-oldest son arrived for freshman ball in 1970 to his glorious senior season of 1973, John, Anne, and Joey, nine years younger than John, rarely missed a game. What they saw unfold, what they lived as a family, remains one of the greatest stories college football has ever told.

The Setting

Cappelletti was a running back and defensive back in high school, but when he joined the Penn State program in 1970, he was unsure how Paterno planned to use him. He preferred carrying the ball, but in that summer's annual Big 33 All-Star Classic, Cappelletti played only on defense, even returning an interception for a touchdown. "Penn State recruited me," he says, "but I'm not sure how highly recruited I was."

In three freshman games, he saw action on both sides of the ball. As a sophomore, somewhat to his chagrin, he played solely in the secondary and also returned punts and kicks. But after the 1971 season, with Lydell Mitchell and Franco Harris headed for the NFL, Paterno needed to fill a backfield void. Open tryouts were held, and Cappelletti impressed the staff throughout the spring while competing against Gary Hayman and highly recruited Tom Donchez. By the

1972 season opener, a 28-21 loss at Tennessee, Cappelletti was Penn State's top rusher.

"I was still learning the position," he says, "and as time went on, I got better and better. There's a lot of experience that comes with repetition, even if it's subconscious. I mean, you run up to the line, and a lot of times you don't remember seeing things, but you make certain cuts off things you see, and it's almost like the path of least resistance for your eyes. You see people blocking or the defense reacting a certain way, and you know you're supposed to go the other way. I think the repetition trains you."

Cappelletti topped 100 yards on the ground five times that season, all games Penn State won en route to a 10-2 mark. After a spring semester during which Paterno seriously flirted with leaving to coach the NFL's New England Patriots, Cappelletti, who would be named co-captain for the 1973 team, returned home to Upper Darby for the summer. It wasn't common then like it is now for players to spend their summers on campus working out as a group to build unity for the coming season. Summer for Cappelletti meant time with family, especially Joey, who, in the previous two years of chemotherapy and spinal taps, had slipped in and out of a coma, spent time in a wheelchair, and had to re-learn how to walk.

John also had a job. In the summer of '73, as he'd done the summer before, Cappelletti ran his own water ice stand at an AM/PM gas station close to his old elementary school's playground. John Sr., then working for Penn Fruit markets, built the stand from scratch. With power and water plus an ice-making machine, Cappelletti earned money selling water ice, sodas, pretzels, and candy to neighborhood kids. (Later, when John went off to the NFL in 1974, his mother lined up employees to man the stand, sending a percentage of the profits to the elementary school.)

When summer ended, Cappelletti rejoined good friends Ed O'Neil, Mark Markovich, Randy Crowder, and a deep core of Penn State seniors and juniors bent on remaining undefeated that fall. As for the Heisman, Cappelletti was just a blip on the preseason watch list. Three months later, he'd all but clinch the storied trophy on a frigid afternoon in Beaver Stadium.

The Game of My Life
By John Cappelletti

PENN STATE VERSUS N.C. STATE
NOVEMBER 10, 1973

Before the 1973 season, I didn't think too much about the Heisman. I didn't think it applied to me all that much. I was mentioned in one preseason magazine. John Morris, the sports information director, might have put some things out, but never the kind of preseason literature I receive today about kids. Yeah, I was coming off a junior season where ultimately I was successful, but I'd had my struggles at the beginning. So I was just looking forward to improving what I could do.

About halfway through that season, Joe Paterno and I had a talk about it. He said the Heisman talk was starting to heat up a little bit, and to just keep doing what we were doing. You take care of the little things, and the big things will take care of themselves.

That year, just like the others before it, my family made it to just about every game, even when my brother wasn't feeling good. He would kind of rally toward the end of the week, knowing there was going to be a game and that he could go to Penn State and go in the locker room. That would get him going. They would all come, but mostly Joey was the only one who would come into the locker room, my father hanging out near the door. Joey knew all the players. He'd go up to them and talk to them, maybe tell them about a play they didn't make or something like that. He got pretty friendly with a few of them.

Afterwards we'd always go out to dinner together as a family. That was the good part. It was so crowded in town, and if somebody would recognize me, it wasn't fun after that. So we used to go out to the Kentucky Fried Chicken on Route 322. It was a little farther outside town, it wasn't crowded, and we would just sit there.

By the time of the N.C. State game, I'd been carrying the ball a lot and we were getting to the point where if I ran the ball a certain number of times, I'd probably get a certain amount of yards. I think

Joe realized that with the weather, he had to rely on the running game a little bit more. In the Maryland game the week before, I'd carried it in the 30s. Against N.C. State, I carried it 41 times.

Lou Holtz and N.C. State had a powerful offense themselves and probably a more unique offense than we were used to seeing as far as the mix of run and pass. We had to control the ball as much as we could to keep them off the field. In fact, I think we realized we were going to have to win the game with our offense that day because our defense was having a tough time against a very talented group of offensive players. I mean, they scored 29 points against our defense, and at that point in the season, it wasn't something we were used to seeing.

It was a pretty physical game. I remember having success on runs of the 5- to 25-yard type. They weren't doing much different as far as bringing people up. And I mean when you have 200-plus yards on the ground, obviously the offensive linemen are creating holes no matter what.

I remember one of the last plays I made was what turned out to be the winning touchdown, from about 25 yards out. I still see the run in my mind every once in a while. At that point there was a little bit of fatigue setting in, and I remember it was a pretty decent run. I recall coming back out of the end zone with Markovich and Tommy Shuman on either side of me. I remember being a little fatigued to the point where they actually kind of put their arms around me.

After the win, I know Lou Holtz made a comment that they might as well have just handed me the Heisman. Cause he thought he was going to come in there and beat an undefeated team at home. And they really did have the team to do it. I just don't think he expected that we were going to be able to run the ball like that.

Game Results

Though unranked at the time, Holtz brought a fearless, offensive-minded squad to Beaver Stadium, and that mentality helped give the Wolfpack an edge in the first half. Plus Penn State did not play like an 8-0 team. With 59,424 fans and scouts from the Orange and Liberty bowls watching intently, the Nittany Lions twice fumbled away potential scoring drives and allowed N.C. State to become the first team to score on the ground against them all season. The Wolfpack led 14-9 at the intermission.

Penn State drove 78 yards in nine plays to start the second half, a 40-yard Shuman-to-Hayman pass setting up a 20-yard Cappelletti touchdown run, his second of the game. A two-point conversion attempt failed, but soon after, Hayman's highlight-reel-worthy, 83-yard punt return made it 22-14.

The Wolfpack, like the bitter cold that eventually brought snow with it that day, would not go away. First N.C. State tied it at 22 on a 70-yard drive. Then, after Bob Nagle's 10-yard touchdown run had put Penn State back on top, N.C. State fullback Charlie Young sprinted 69 yards to pay dirt to even matters again: 29 all.

That's when Cappy took over. He carried the ball four times in a 60-yard drive, lighting up the scoreboard for a third time on a 27-yard rumble. Though Matt Bahr missed the extra point, the Lions' defense rose to the occasion on N.C. State's final two drives. The Pack punted once, and on the game's final possession, PSU's Jim Bradley batted down a fourth-down pass with two seconds left to clinch the win. The scoreboard read 35-29 Penn State.

Cappelletti's 41 carries remains a Penn State single-game record; his 220 rushing yards were a career high. A week later, again at Beaver Stadium, number 22 scored four touchdowns—the last coming after good friend Markovich lobbied Paterno to put Cappy back in the game—in a 49-10 rout of Ohio University. Markovich knew a month earlier that John, at Joey's asking, had promised his little brother a four-touchdown day as a birthday gift. "He picked four, not me," John says. "I don't know why. Maybe after seeing me score three, he thought, 'Well, you scored three already. That's not going to be anything special.'"

Eleven-year-old Joey was there that day against Ohio, just as he was on November 24 when State made it 11-0 with a 35-13 defeat of Pitt, and on December 13 when his big brother dedicated the Heisman Trophy to him. John's emotional speech—"He puts up with much more than I'll ever put up with," he said, "and I think this trophy is more his than mine because he has been a great inspiration to me"—was not planned. It wasn't even written down. It came from the heart, not the notes he'd scribbled earlier on an index card while dressing for the ceremony in his room at the Downtown Athletic Club.

"I have vivid memories," says Cappelletti, who was taping the *Bob Hope All-American Football Show* when he first learned he'd won the Heisman, "a pretty good snapshot of being on the dais, where my parents were and where Joey was. Maybe because it was emotional it gets a little more ingrained in the memory.

"It obviously moved people, people who had had similar situations or knew of someone in a similar situation, relating to a young child being sick and a family dealing with it. And I remember the quote from [Archbishop] Fulton Sheen afterwards. ("Maybe, for the first time in your lives, you have heard a speech from the heart and not from the lips. Part of John's triumph was made by Joseph's sorrow. You don't need a blessing. God has already blessed you in John Cappelletti.") That was quite something. I was thinking to myself, now I gotta live with this the rest of my life, an archbishop saying this about me? I can't mess this up. But for him to say that was like the perfect ending to the whole night."

Reflecting on State

The Heisman Trophy returned to Upper Darby that December, and there it remained for years, long after Joey passed away in 1976 at age 13, with John at his bedside. The statue itself is now with John in California, but the weight of the bronze material feathers in comparison to the impact Cappelletti's tale has had on football, on athletics, on the world, really.

Thanks largely to a successful book and movie—*Something For Joey*—Cappelletti has spent the last 32 years fielding letters, e-mails, and calls, each from someone somewhere who benefited uniquely from reading or viewing the story. "I get them from Mexico, China, Canada," says Cappelletti, who left State in '74 with a degree in law enforcement and correction. "It's unbelievable the impact this has had and sustained over time. Even last year a group of fourth-graders in Japan wrote me. It makes you feel good, cause when you read the letters, you see what the kids are getting out of it, whether it's their relationship with their brother, sister, or grandparents.

"When I was playing in the NFL [he retired in 1983] it got to be, well, is this ever gonna stop? As I've gotten older, I've seen the value in all this, the good it does. The memory is kept alive. Sometimes it makes all the difference in whether people can go forward in life or not."

Today Cappelletti has four boys of his own with wife Betty: Nicholas, John, Thomas, and youngest son Joseph. Says John of naming his son after his late brother: "I didn't know they were going to be all boys, but when we got to that point, it just seemed like the right thing to do. I talked to my parents about it, and they were happy."

Cappelletti went from the NFL to the construction business to commercial real estate to his current role as a partner at AlphaBio, which produces custom process equipment for firms in the biotech and pharmaceutical industries. He flies east several times a year for business, family visits, Homecoming in State College, or the Heisman ceremony in New York City. Life rolls on for John Cappelletti.

"You still have to deal with all the real situations in life: grades, sports, discipline, whatever for your own family," he says. "But sometimes I look back and see everything that's been accomplished. Then you look at your life and say, jeez, a movie was made about my life. How did that happen?"

10

TODD BLACKLEDGE

NAME: Todd Alan Blackledge
BORN: February 25, 1961, in Canton, Ohio
HOMETOWN: North Canton, Ohio
CURRENT RESIDENCE: Canton, Ohio
OCCUPATION: ESPN college football analyst; former NFL player
POSITION: Quarterback
HEIGHT: 6 feet, 3 inches
PLAYING WEIGHT: 225 pounds
YEARS LETTERED: 1980 to 1982
NUMBER WORN AT PSU: 14
ACCOMPLISHMENTS: Led Penn State in passing each year from 1980 to '82, throwing for 2,218 yards in '82, still the fifth-highest single-season total in school history; 22 touchdowns that season are a PSU single-season record; had 41 career passing TDs, tied with Tony Sacca for most in school history; led Nittany Lions to national title in 1983 Sugar Bowl, claiming Most Outstanding Player honors; also won Davey O'Brien Award as nation's top quarterback and finished sixth in that year's Heisman balloting; first-round pick of Kansas City Chiefs in '83 NFL draft; played five seasons with Chiefs, two with Pittsburgh Steelers; 1982 Academic All-American inducted into GTE Academic All-America Hall of Fame in 1997; became ESPN's *College Football Saturday Primetime* analyst in 2006 after seven years as CBS' lead college football analyst and earlier on-air stints with ABC Sports and the Big East Network.
THE GAME: Penn State at Pitt, November 28, 1981

The Young Life of
Todd Blackledge

Todd Blackledge was born in Canton, Ohio, not far from the Pro Football Hall of Fame. His father, Ron, has spent a lifetime coaching football players of all ages. But when Todd, Ron's only son, reached his teen years in the mid-1970s, he had his heart set on firing jump shots, not spirals. Specifically, the kid wanted to play college basketball at the University of Kentucky. "If I could have picked what I wanted to do," Blackledge says, "that would have been it."

Ron supported his son's dream, much the way his wife and children had backed his moves up the football ladder. Ron went from coaching high school ball in Ohio to his first college assistant job, at Cincinnati, and when Todd was in elementary school, Ron became Kentucky's offensive line coach. The Blackledges (Todd has two younger sisters) moved to Lexington, Kentucky, where Todd attended Tates Creek elementary and junior high schools, dreaming endlessly of someday playing Wildcats basketball.

Ron's transfers continued. After Todd's freshman year of high school, the family left Kentucky for Princeton, New Jersey, where Ron took an assistant job with the Ivy League Tigers. A year later they hit the road again, this time back to Ohio, where Ron was hired as offensive coordinator at Kent. It was a lateral move career-wise for Ron, but part of the draw was a chance to re-immerse Todd in devout high school football culture, the stuff of pep bands and jammed bleachers and games staged under Friday night lights.

It wasn't that Ron was trying to discourage Todd from pursuing basketball over football. In fact he often gathered rebounds for his son during driveway shootarounds, or threw batting practice to Todd, who was a decent baseball player, too. No, the decision on what sport to pursue was left to Todd, and he reached that decision in 1978, the summer after his junior year at North Canton High. A 6-foot-3 post player, he was invited to the B.C. All-Star Camp in Milledgeville, Georgia, where he mixed it up with the likes of future NBAers Ralph Sampson, Dominique Wilkins, and 250 other talents, many of them taller, quicker, with niftier dribbling abilities and better hops. "It was

While Todd Blackledge won MVP honors for his starring role in Penn State's upset of Georgia in the 1983 Sugar Bowl, his finest hour may have come one season earlier when he outgunned Pitt quarterback Dan Marino to help Penn State upset the then No. 1-ranked Panthers at Pitt Stadium.

a real eye-opening experience," Blackledge says. "There were guys who were 6-foot-7, 6-foot-8, 6-foot-9 who could do everything I could do in terms of shooting and ball handling. I came back that summer with a new passion for football."

Despite possessing a strong arm, Blackledge had only started playing quarterback his freshman year of high school. Then, three years later, when he realized his ticket to a Division I scholarship rode on his right arm, he looked south again, initially considering SEC powers Tennessee and Alabama. He later narrowed his search to four schools—Penn State, Michigan State, Notre Dame, and Tennessee—each of which offered him full rides.

He visited Penn State then Michigan State, where he watched Magic Johnson and the Spartans hoops team and took a liking to football coach Darrell Rogers. Penn State? The Nittany Lions had a great campus, a great throwing quarterback in Chuck Fusina (a rarity for traditionally run-heavy Penn State), and a great coach in Joe Paterno, who hit it off with the Blackledges, especially Todd's Italian grandfather.

"Joe sat in my living room and told me he thought I was a quarterback who could help lead them to a national championship," Blackledge says of the conversation that led him to select Penn State. "Four years after that, we did just that."

The Setting

Paterno wasn't messing around. When 18-year-old Blackledge arrived in State College to prepare for his freshman year, he found a wide-open depth chart. Senior Dayle Tate, who'd backed up Fusina the year before, was first string, but Paterno was intent on grooming Blackledge and fellow newcomer Jeff Hostetler to be ready and ready soon. A smart, likeable kid with good instincts and a penchant for buoying his teammates, Blackledge found himself running long pass play situations and two-minute drills in practice. But in the team's final scrimmage before the '79 season opener, he broke a bone in his throwing hand.

The untimely injury cost Blackledge his entire freshman year, a year in which the Nittany Lions of Matt Millen and Bruce Clark went 8-4, including a Liberty Bowl win against Tulane. His cast came off late that fall, giving Blackledge plenty of time to prep for spring ball. Tate was out of the picture by then, and though upperclassman Frank Rocco was still in it, most within the program knew either Hostetler or Blackledge would start come September. "He and I were competing through the spring and all the way through to August," Blackledge says. "Joe didn't decide who was going to start until the Thursday of the first week of the season."

It was Hostetler. Well, for three games at least. Hostetler, a legacy at State—older brothers Doug and Ron both lettered there—led the Lions to a 2-0 start in 1980, but he struggled in Game 3, a home contest against No. 3 Nebraska. Looking for a spark versus the Cornhuskers, Paterno subbed in Blackledge, who played well enough in Joe's eyes to earn a start the ensuing week at undefeated Missouri. Blackledge did not disappoint, scrambling for two scores and tossing another in a 29-21 win. Paterno had his man, and Blackledge had the starter's job. Hostetler, who years later quarterbacked the NFL's New York Giants to victory in Super Bowl XXV, transferred to West Virginia after the 1980 season.

"It was difficult in some ways," Blackledge says, "but there's always competition, and that's just the way it is. Things ended up working out great for him and ultimately great for me."

With Hostetler gone, Blackledge settled into a leadership role, growing ever more comfortable with an atypically aerial-friendly Penn State offense and a gang of teammates and buddies high on talent and higher on chemistry. Of course, many in Nittany Lion Nation, Blackledge included, point to chemistry as the difference-maker in Penn State winning the national title in the 1983 Sugar Bowl. But Blackledge also knows that the 1982 season would never have happened without 1981. That was the year a redshirt sophomore signal-caller and his roommate/best friend/top running back, Curt Warner, carried Penn State to a 6-0 start, then saw the Lions lose two of three only to rediscover themselves in a closing stretch capped by an unforgettable late-November rout of Dan Marino-led Pitt.

The Game of My Life
By Todd Blackledge

PENN STATE AT PITT
NOVEMBER 28, 1981

I expected to win every game I ever played. You have to. And in 1981, I knew we had a really great team. We just had not played up to our potential a couple times. There was the loss [17-14] to Miami when we were ranked No. 1. They weren't as good as we were, but we let them hang around. When you do that, they start getting confidence and become tougher and tougher to beat. And then in the Alabama game [a 31-16 home setback], we did not play well. That was an ugly loss.

That Pitt game was a chance to redeem the season. Because up to that point, I think we really had underachieved. The team had the kind of talent that was capable of bigger things, and here we were with two losses, and now we were playing the undefeated, No. 1-ranked team in the country at their place.

It was a crazy game. For starters, Dan Marino had had such a phenomenal junior season: he had thrown 30-some touchdown passes. Their offense was beautiful; I mean, it was something to behold. And when we started that game, they went up 14-0, and we couldn't even begin to stop them. They were going up and down the field on us.

Meanwhile, we couldn't do anything on offense. At the end of the first quarter we had minus-1 yard of total offense. Then came the play that turned the tide. They were on their way in to score again, when Dan threw a post pattern, and it was intercepted by Roger Jackson. We didn't score on that next possession, but we ultimately did score twice before halftime to make it 14-14.

The whole game turned in the second half. Their strategy was to play us straight man to man and crowd the line of scrimmage to stop our run. When you read that coverage, especially when you know you have enough blockers to give you time, you're going to be able to make some big plays. That's the risk of blitzing and playing man to man.

Even if you have a guy covered, if he makes the catch and you miss the tackle, it still turns into a big play. And that's what happened a couple times. One play Kenny Jackson made a catch, made a guy miss, and turned it into a touchdown.

Momentum is a crazy thing. There was kind of a helpless feeling early on in the first quarter when we couldn't do anything. Then the game really turned, and it steamrolled in the second half. Part of it was they weren't able to protect the ball, and we got the ball in good field position a couple times. We also were able to make some big plays. And everything bounced our way in the second half. On one of our touchdowns, we fumbled the ball, it went into the end zone, and one of our linemen fell on it.

To win a game in that fashion, in their place the Friday after Thanksgiving when they were No. 1, it was pretty awesome. I remember toward the end of the game, the Blue Band played "Another One Bites the Dust" and then "Happy Birthday." It was [Pitt coach] Jackie Sherrill's birthday that day. And after the game, Joe let guys who were from that area stay in town; we didn't all have to go back to State College. I remember I stayed overnight and went to dinner at Klein's Seafood. A lot of people recognized us and came up to talk about the game. Then I went to the Steelers game the next day, and I remember getting my picture taken with Terry Bradshaw in the locker room. It was a pretty special weekend for me.

Game Results

Among the 60,260 fans pulling for the home team at Pitt Stadium on November 28, 1981, few were surprised to see the Panthers jump out to a 14-0 lead on Penn State. This was how Danny Marino & Co. had done it all season. In fact, No. 1 Pitt had won 17 straight on the back of a high-octane aerial assault, and the national title was in reach. But miscues changed everything.

After Marino tossed his 33rd and 34th touchdowns of the season, both to Dwight Collins, in the game's first 10 minutes, the junior quarterback lobbed a pass to the corner of the end zone, intended for

Collins again. This time Penn State cornerback Roger Jackson picked it off, the first of what would be four Marino interceptions on the day. The stop gave the Nittany Lions hope, and at 11:55 of the second quarter, fullback Mike Meade put the Lions on the board with a 2-yard run. Two series later, after swapping turnovers, Blackledge scored on a draw from 8 yards out, a touchdown set up by a 52-yard Blackledge-to-Kenny Jackson strike. It was 14 all at the half.

Pitt fell apart in the third quarter. Bill Beach fumbled on the opening possession of the second half, and three plays later Blackledge hit Jackson with another bomb. This time the wideout snared the pass at the 10, whirled 360 degrees, and beat two defenders to the end zone. Minutes later, the Blackledge-Jackson battery struck again, this time for 45 yards and a 28-14 lead.

Brian Franco later tacked on two field goals for State, who also got two picks from sophomore safety Mark Robinson, including one he returned 91 yards for a touchdown. Guard Sean Farrell even scored, recovering a Warner fumble in the end zone. When night fell on State's 48-14 upset, Paterno had his 150th career win and arguably the greatest upset of his head-coaching career. "We can't cry," said Marino, whose Panthers committed seven turnovers. "We just made too many mistakes, and you can't win with so many fumbles, penalties, and interceptions."

The victory was particularly sweet for Blackledge, who'd faced comparisons to Marino all week in the press, and wound up more than holding his own with 262 passing yards and two touchdown tosses. "This was the best game of my life," he said that night.

Twenty-five years have given Blackledge perspective. The Pitt upset can't rival the Sugar Bowl that was played 14 months later, but it's equally momentous for him when seen as a stepping stone for the magical 1982 season. "Beating Pitt and then USC in the Fiesta Bowl were good wins to end on," Blackledge says. "I think some of that season's missed opportunity fueled us in the summer for the guys who were coming back. Cause a lot of people thought the next year would be a rebuilding year for us. But it ended up coming together."

Reflecting on State

Much has come together for Blackledge in his years since State. In 1982, after debating his options, he passed up his final year of eligibility at PSU to enter the NFL draft. Today he says that given the chance to do it again, he would have returned for his senior season to captain the 1983 squad. But it worked out well at the time. Blackledge went in the first round to the Kansas City Chiefs, part of a superb crop of drafted quarterbacks including Marino, Jim Kelly, and John Elway.

Blackledge's pro career didn't result in the success of which little boys dream. The second of six quarterbacks taken in the first round that year, he was the last of the six to start. In his seven-year career, he completed just 48.1 percent of his passes and threw only 29 touchdowns. On the upside, his career gave him enough exposure to grow as a television analyst.

The speech communication major with a 3.8 grade-point average broke in with talk shows in Cleveland and Canton, moved to preseason NFL games and NCAA bowl games on ESPN, then to the Big East Network. He went from ABC to CBS in 1999, where he covered SEC football for seven years before moving to ESPN in 2006 as an analyst on ESPN's *College Football Saturday Primetime*. He also handles some *College GameDay*, *SportsCenter*, and ESPN Radio duties.

"I love college football, I love the environment," says Blackledge, who with wife Cherie has four boys between ages three and 10. "I love the feeling of game day, of waking up in a hotel within walking distance of the stadium, the buzz around campus, and the feeling in the stadium. I love going to college towns and finding the little hole-in-the-wall places to eat. Some guys in broadcasting, they don't like the college circuit because there aren't many Ritz Carltons in Tuscaloosa, Alabama. But I love the whole feel of it."

Falls for the Blackledges are usually too busy for return trips to central Pennsylvania, but he has taken his three oldest sons to State College for Blue-White weekend. On those rides home, he can always reflect on the trip he and his teammates made a quarter-century ago to rout a rival and set Penn State on course for its first national title.

"One of my great disappointments," he says wistfully, "is that the Pitt-Penn State game is gone. I thought that was as good a rivalry as any in college football."

Gone? For now. Forgotten? Never.

11

MIKE MUNCHAK

NAME: Michael Anthony Munchak
BORN: March 5, 1960, in Scranton, Pennsylvania
HOMETOWN: Scranton, Pennsylvania
CURRENT RESIDENCE: Nashville, Tennessee
OCCUPATION: Offensive line coach for Tennessee Titans; former NFL player
COLLEGE POSITION: Guard
HEIGHT: 6 feet, 3 inches
PLAYING WEIGHT: 257 pounds
YEARS LETTERED: 1978-79, 1981
NUMBER WORN AT PSU: 78
ACCOMPLISHMENTS: Second-team All-American as redshirt junior in 1981; first offensive lineman (eighth overall) selected in 1982 NFL draft; earned starting left guard job as rookie with Houston Oilers; made first- or second-team All-Pro 10 times; elected to nine Pro Bowls; played in 159 career games; had number 63 retired by Oilers; elected to Pro Football Hall of Fame as part of Class of 2001, becoming 27th offensive lineman—and fifth Nittany Lion—ever to make the pro hall.
THE GAME: The Fiesta Bowl, Penn State versus USC, January 1, 1982

The Young Life of Mike Munchak

Mike Munchak addresses life as it comes. It's been that way since he was a kid in Scranton, delivering the *Scranton Times* afternoon edition on foot, pumping coins into pinball machines at Nay Aug Park, or battling his five sisters for bathroom time in his parents' one-and-a-half-bath home. It was the same with sports, from one-on-one hoops in his back alley to pickup football in the snow-filled street. "I never thought past the time I was enjoying right then, and what I was competing to do," says the Pro Football Hall of Famer. "I never thought how this affected that. I thought, just do the right thing."

When decisions needed to be made, he made them. When sports began conflicting with his paper route, he subcontracted his sisters to cover the 65-customer route. Organized football? He discovered an opportunity to play at eight years old, then convinced his mother, Paula, to let him become a Central City Indian. ("I think all the sad eyes got to her," he says.) The next year several neighborhood fathers—including his dad, Mike—started the East Scranton Apollos football team. Mike Sr. was a truck driver who would work 12 hours then rush home to practices.

One particular memory from his time with the Apollos still brings a smile to Munchak's face: "I remember they put me at linebacker against nine- and 10-year-olds. One of the bigger kids had the ball, and I tackled him. I was in the pile next to him and he said, 'Listen, if you broke my helmet, you're dead.' Kids then had plastic helmets. Thankfully his helmet wasn't harmed."

By seventh grade, Munchak had outgrown the 120-pound Apollos weight limit. By high school, he'd hit 6 foot, 2 inches and 195 pounds. And though basketball was his first love, he excelled as a hard-nosed fullback/defensive end at Scranton Central High. Recruiters noticed. "After my junior year, I knew I wasn't going anywhere with basketball cause I didn't have the height to be an inside guy on the next level, and I couldn't handle the ball," says Munchak, who rushed for nearly 800 yards his senior football season. "But I thought I had a shot in football to earn a scholarship, maybe go to a small school."

Shortly after Mike Munchak and Penn State's offensive line sprung running back Curt Warner for 145 yards and two scores in a Fiesta Bowl showdown with Marcus Allen's USC Trojans, the Scranton, Pennsylvania, native passed up his final season of eligibility and became the first offensive lineman selected in the 1982 NFL draft.

He was right about the free ride, but in 1977, big fish were jumping too for the 235-pound back with natural lower-body strength. Penn State felt it had an in-state recruiting advantage, and early on it did, considering Munchak didn't want to go far from home. But after visiting several schools, he figured he'd have a better chance to play at Syracuse or Maryland than Penn State. (Tom Coughlin, the Syracuse assistant who recruited Munchak, was the first to project Munchak as an offensive lineman in college.) When Penn State learned Munchak was not a lock, alarms went off.

"The phone rings and it's Joe [Paterno]," Munchak says. "I'm like stuttering. He goes, 'Mike, did we handle something incorrectly?' I said, 'No Coach, I'm just thinking where I might fit best.' He says, 'I'll tell you what, are your parents going to be home tomorrow? Why don't you ask your mother if it's okay if I stop by?'"

The answer, of course, was yes. Like a script replayed hundreds of times, Paterno arrived at the Munchaks' for dinner, "and when he left," Mike says, "I knew I was gonna go there."

It was a wild sequence. "I was thinking, 'Oh my God, I can't believe they're gonna give me a scholarship there,'" says Munchak, who then already had an older sister enrolled at PSU. "I'm sure a lot of people in my hometown thought the same thing. Cause I was a good player, but being a good player in Scranton is a little different than getting a scholarship to Penn State. I was in awe of it."

The Setting

If Munchak was in awe, he didn't show it. At the first meeting before the 1978 season, Munchak walked in, sat on the defensive side of the room, and waited for a playbook that never came. Eventually assistant Dick Anderson retrieved him and told him he was a tight end. Munchak sat in one meeting as a tight end, ran through a 45-minute workout, and arrived at practice the next day to find a note that Paterno wanted to see him.

"Coach, I had a note to see you?" said Munchak.

"Yeah," replied Paterno. "We're moving you. Turn your playbook in. We have another book for you. We're moving you to defensive line. That all right? You have a problem?"

"No. I just thought I was going to play tight end," said Munchak.

"You can't play tight end," replied the coach.

"I can," responded Munchak. "I really didn't get a chance to do anything yet."

"That practice yesterday?" said Paterno. "I saw you running routes. You can't play tight end."

The shifting had just begun. After 10 days on defensive line—he spent practices learning from Bruce Clark and Matt Millen—Munchak was moved to tackle to fill offensive line depth. He also played special teams and traveled with a talented squad that would go undefeated in '78 before losing to Alabama in the Sugar Bowl.

"I remember calling my parents after the first week, thinking I made a mistake," he says. "What am I doing? Just cause of position changes. I was thinking I'm not going to fit in anywhere. Then, all of a sudden within the same year, I remember being on one of the buses at one of the away games thinking, 'I fit in here. This is where I belong.'"

Not that the position shuffling was over. Though he'd been told he could try defense again if he so desired, Munchak, then weighing 250 pounds, was moved to center in the spring of '79. A week later, satisfied he could play center, the staff switched him to guard, where he'd start that fall on first team opposite Sean Farrell, another defensive lineman turned guard.

In the ensuing 12 months, two things happened that would have key impacts on Munchak's career. First, he became a student of Dick Anderson's, who preached technique. When he'd finish off successful blocks, Munchak would hear complaints about footwork from his perfectionist line coach. "You obviously need strength and athleticism," Munchak says, "but a coach can't do much about those two things. So you concentrate on technique, demeanor, and all that."

The second key impact on his career was injury. In a spring drill before his junior season, Munchak hurt his left knee, requiring arthroscopic surgery during the summer of 1980. Recovery was supposed to take six weeks, but when training camp started, he was still in pain. So he underwent a second procedure to remove much of the knee's cartilage, which forced him to redshirt the season. (Knee pains plagued Munchak as a pro, too; by late in his career, he'd skip practice, play in games, then ice his knees for hours.)

"When I had the second one done, that was probably the most depressed I was in my life to that point," he recalls. "It was hard watching those guys play and me not be part of it. I went from starting to thinking, 'I'm not sure if I'll be able to mend this knee. I may never come back.'"

He did return to the field for the '81 season, but by then, fear of reinjury and unity with his recruiting class had him thinking this might be his final year of college ball. When the 1982 Fiesta Bowl approached, Munchak wondered whether it would be his last game in a Penn State uniform.

The Game of My Life
By Mike Munchak

THE FIESTA BOWL
PENN STATE VERSUS USC
JANUARY 1, 1982

In 1981 we thought we were gonna take it all, and a lot of others thought the same thing. We'd all been freshmen when we were No. 1 for 10 weeks and lost to Alabama, so we knew what that was like. We had a tough schedule, but we felt great about it.

We had a great mix of guys on the offensive line: me, Sean Farrell, Pete Speros, Jim Romano, Julius Contz—big Julius. We were very familiar with each other. We were dedicated to it. And we were gonna be a big part of how things went that year.

I remember the Miami loss well. Playing in that storming rain, we couldn't get the points on the board. We blew that game down there. I think we knew once we lost one, we were screwed. We had a hangover from that one, from dealing with that loss, and we didn't handle it very well against Alabama. To lose at home? No way.

But we regrouped. I think Joe did a great job of pulling us together and not letting this thing fall apart. And we went and put it on Notre Dame and beat Pitt at Pitt, which was a huge win. It was a tale of a couple seasons there, and we ended on a positive note and still felt good about ourselves.

As for me, I didn't talk to agents or anything, but I was talking to people who had some knowledge of whether I should think of coming out. Is it totally silly to consider this? Can I get drafted in a position where it made sense to do it? My thinking was, I came in with these guys as freshmen, and I wanted to go out with them. This is my class.

Then the injury thing sunk in. What if I hurt the knee again? Then what happens? Plus I was going to graduate with my degree. So I talked to Joe about it during the dead time before the bowl when we weren't practicing. We talked briefly about my options if I stayed, some of the recognition you get by being a senior and how much they wanted me to be a part of it. I knew that.

I also knew that after the USC game, I'd have two or three days to make a decision. Rosters for the senior bowls were already determined, but they had this Olympia Gold Bowl that year, the only year they had it, and I felt I could help my stock in the draft by practicing against some of the best players.

On Fiesta Bowl game day, our war cry was that our class was going out, we want to win, we want to hammer USC. [USC was] disappointed like us. They thought they were gonna be in the Rose Bowl. We thought we'd be in the championship game or No. 1. We knew we weren't, but we still wanted to do well. USC seemed more disappointed to be there. The Fiesta Bowl wasn't doing it for them.

The other thing that motivated us was Marcus Allen being the Heisman winner. They had Marcus, we had Curt Warner. Our thinking was, Curt Warner's gonna outshine the Heisman Trophy winner. So the defense was motivated to shut down Marcus and the offensive line wanted to show that the best running back that day was on our sideline.

I think the first two times Curt touched the ball, he scored. We ran one of our pull plays, the guards pulled, and we led him out there. They were two nice runs. On defense, Chet Parlevecchio was our team captain—a very vocal guy. [USC offensive lineman] Bruce Matthews (later a teammate of Munchak's with the Oilers) used to tell me Chet was calling Marcus Allen, "Marc." "Hey, Marc! It's not your day, Marc!" Bruce is going, "Who's Marc?"

Bruce, Leo Wisnewski, Roy Foster, Joey Browner, Chip Banks…there were a lot of great players on the field that day. But I think we wanted it a lot more than they did. It was big for us to go out with a win and for Curt to have a big day. And our defense took a heck of a lot of pride in shutting Allen down. If we'd won but Marcus had had a huge game, I think our guys would have been depressed.

After the game I still had two or three days to make a decision. Ultimately I went back to Joe and told him. I think he was a little shocked I'd leave. But he handled it very professionally, said we'd love to have you, and made the case. I said, "Coach, in my mind, you have a great team with or without me."

And of course, the next year they beat Georgia for the title. I remember watching all those games. We were on strike that year, my first year in the NFL, and I wasn't even playing. But I never remember looking at it and saying I felt I should have stayed, because I felt so good about what I did. At the time it was just right to go out with my class.

Still, I would have loved to have been there. I would be lying to say I wouldn't have wanted to win it or been there for that. … But that was their time and that was for them, and I felt like I was still part of it.

Game Results

Penn State's New Year's Day 1982 clash with USC was just the second meeting in the history of the storied programs, the previous one coming in the 1923 Rose Bowl. Both teams had higher expectations: Penn State's midseason losses to Miami and Alabama removed it from title contention, while the Trojans were derailed by losses to Arizona and Rose Bowl-bound Washington.

That day USC might have held a crowd advantage—more of the 71,053 in Tempe's Sun Devil Stadium were Trojans faithful—but Penn State was rolling off late-season wins over Notre Dame and Pitt. Paterno had his troops jacked. On the first play from scrimmage, State's Dave Opfar hit Heisman Trophy winner Marcus Allen in the backfield and stripped him of the ball, which the Lions recovered at USC's 17-yard line. Two plays later Warner scored his first of two touchdowns on the day, sprinting off tackle to make it 7-0.

USC tied it late in the first when All-American linebacker Chip Banks picked off an errant Todd Blackledge pass and returned it 20 yards for a touchdown. But the tie didn't last, as minutes later, Blackledge hit wideout Greg Garrity with a 52-yard TD strike to make it 14-7.

It was more of the same in the second half, with Penn State driving 80 yards on the half's opening possession and scoring on a 21-yard Warner dash. That was more than enough for a ferocious Lions defense, which swarmed Allen, bursting into the Trojan backfield for 11 tackles for a loss (six sacks) on the night while collecting three interceptions.

Even before the gun sounded on a 26-10 Penn State victory, NBC had cut away to Rose Bowl coverage. When it was over, Warner had outrushed Allen 145 yards to 85, the Heisman winner's worst output of the year.

"Sorry we couldn't give you a better game, Joe," USC coach John Robinson told Paterno when the coaches met at midfield afterwards.

Said Paterno to the press: "We feel we could probably beat any team in the country right now. That doesn't mean we'll be voted the best team." As it was, State finished the year No. 3 behind Texas and No. 1 Clemson. Paterno's elusive first championship was still one year away.

Reflecting on State

It's been nearly 25 years since Mike Munchak played his final collegiate contest, yet he remains quick to credit his days there for his success since. "At Penn State they educated you in why you were doing it, so you understood and enjoyed it more," says the seven-time All-AFC pick, who earned Houston's starting left guard job as a rookie in 1982 and helped the Oilers make the playoffs every year from 1987 through 1993. "You got more out of it. It wasn't, 'Go block that guy.' It was, 'Here's how we're doing it, here's why we're doing it, here's how I want you to do it—learn it all.' So when I got to the NFL, I thought I was way ahead of some guys because they weren't taught the way I was."

Munchak speaks fondly of Paterno for having set boundaries and consequences for players who crossed them. It was a structured system within which he thrived, and it's the same brand of discipline he uses today with young Tennessee Titans offensive linemen he coaches. That attention to detail in footwork and technique instilled in him by Dick Anderson? It's also part of Munchak's approach to coaching.

"Other than getting married to my wife," says the father of two, "going to Penn State is probably the best decision I've made."

The business logistics major at PSU never expected to wind up coaching. But when friends and colleagues urged him to consider the profession, it was an easy sell. "I knew I'd love it," he says. "I really enjoy working with the position because I know it well and feel like I can help these guys a lot. That's what I'm in it for. It's like having a bunch of sons.

"With these jobs, if you're not winning, they want to make changes," he continues. "It's a tough little business. But we've been blessed. We haven't had to move. I've been playing or coaching with the same organization for jeez, almost 25 years."

He's been blessed in many ways.

12

GREGG
GARRITY

NAME: Gregg David Garrity
BORN: November 24, 1960, in Pittsburgh, Pennsylvania
HOMETOWN: Bradford Woods, Pennsylvania
CURRENT RESIDENCE: Bradford Woods, Pennsylvania
OCCUPATION: Owner of All Hands On Deck renovation firm;
former NFL player
POSITION: Wide receiver
HEIGHT: 5 feet, 10 inches
PLAYING WEIGHT: 165 pounds
YEARS LETTERED: 1979 to 1982
NUMBER WORN AT PSU: 19
ACCOMPLISHMENTS: Led Penn State in receptions in 1981 (23
catches for 415 yards); had best receiving game of career in
1983 Sugar Bowl, grabbing four passes for 116 yards;
became just the second Penn State player ever featured on
cover of *Sports Illustrated* in January 10, 1983, issue; selected
in fifth round of 1983 NFL draft by Pittsburgh Steelers; played
seven pro seasons with Steelers and Philadelphia Eagles.
THE GAME: The Sugar Bowl, Penn State versus Georgia,
January 1, 1983

The Young Life of Gregg Garrity

Gregg Garrity never looked much like a football player growing up, and if you saw him today, you wouldn't peg him as one of the most famous players in Penn State history. But size, at least in Garrity's football career, never really mattered.

The second youngest of five children, Garrity was one of the skinniest kids growing up in his Western Pennsylvania neighborhood of Bradford Woods. Even though his father, Jim, had been a two-way player at Penn State and co-captain of the 1954 Nittany Lions, it appeared early on that Gregg's only chance to follow in his dad's footsteps would require a major growth spurt. On the upside, the kid could always run. When Garrity began playing midget football at age seven, he was compact but slippery. "If you have speed," he says, "once you get around the corner, you're home free."

Garrity proved that size didn't matter at North Allegheny High School. He was 5 feet, 9 inches and 135 pounds. He looked more at home running the 4x100-meter relay—his relay team set a state record that stood for nearly two decades—than catching passes in pads. Football, however, was Garrity's true love, and not because his father pressured him to play.

"My parents were very supportive in everything," says Garrity, whose father was also Joe Paterno's first recruit as an assistant at Penn State. Gregg's mother, Gail, and his maternal grandmother also attended State. "They never forced us to do anything," he continues, referring to his parents. "The only thing they instilled in us is once you start something, you have to finish it. You can't quit. Sometimes you have some bad times in sports, but if you weren't impulsive and [instead] rode it out, something good could happen later."

A sure-tackling, stiff-hitting safety in high school, Garrity hoped his speed would earn him looks from Division I-A programs. But all his 4.3 40 time earned him was rejection. And dejection. Syracuse said he was too small. Despite a family connection with West Virginia athletic director Ed Pastilong, Mountaineers coach Frank Signetti wanted Garrity to try military school for two years. Even Kent State,

Gregg Garrity proved throughout his college career that size didn't matter. For the undersized wide receiver, simply reaching the national title game stage in 1983 was the culmination of an improbable journey.

then coached by Ron Blackledge (father of future Nittany Lion quarterback Todd), took a pass.

Jim Garrity also sent tapes of Gregg to Paterno, who eventually agreed to have Gregg visit campus in 1979. "My dad and I went up and met with Joe and walked around," Gregg says. "He showed me the weight room, and there's two guys sitting in there, Bruce Clark and Matt Millen. I'm like, 'Oh man, these guys are houses!' They weighed 100 pounds more than I did. I was like, 'You gotta be kidding me.'"

But Paterno had an offer, and he wasn't kidding. "He said, 'Come here as a walk-on and you'll come up when the scholarship guys come up,'" Garrity recalls. "'You'll do everything they do except your parents have to pay the bill.'"

Garrity pondered it, discussed it with his father, then, despite one competing offer to play at Clarion, he accepted Paterno's scenario. He'd be guaranteed a roster spot, but the rest was up to him.

The Setting

Garrity had never played a down at wide receiver in his brief football career when he arrived in University Park in 1979. That first year was no different. Though Garrity saw most of his action on special teams, he moved up to second string in the secondary when academic troubles befell defensive backs Pete Harris and Karl McCoy. He was still undersized, but there he was, playing football at his dad's alma mater.

Shortly after Penn State's 9-6 win against Tulane in that year's Liberty Bowl, Garrity met privately with Paterno to ask for a scholarship. "Joe had said, 'If you prove to me and the coaches you can play Division I football, we'll give you a scholarship,'" Garrity says. "I said, 'I think I proved to everybody that I can play.'"

There were no rides available at the moment, but Paterno said he'd work on it. In the meantime, he and the staff had a plan for Garrity—a move to wide receiver. He had burner's speed. He had good hands. Plus, it was only an experiment. If it failed, Garrity could always return to defense.

As it went, he never looked back. In the 1980 Blue-White spring game, Garrity caught a pass across the middle, made for the sideline, turned upfield and beat every defender to the end zone. What he didn't know about the position—"I was a blank slate out there," Garrity admits—receivers coach Booker Brooks began teaching him.

Forget that in 1980 Garrity was maybe 165 pounds dripping wet, or that his hands, while sure, were some of the smallest on the team. He soaked up everything, including Brooks' mantra that when running crossing routes, an unavoidable collision would hurt a lot less if you hung onto the ball.

Within a year, Garrity had developed into a prototypical possession receiver, save for that 4.3 40 speed he could turn to when situations called for something deep. He caught practically everything chucked his way during the 1981 season and finished with a team-best 23 grabs for 415 yards. His 52-yard touchdown catch in the 1982 Fiesta Bowl gave State the lead for good in a 26-10 pounding of USC. Of course, on the rare occasion he did drop a pass that season, even in practice, Paterno was all over him.

"He could be on the defensive field, and you'd drop a ball, and he'd run 60, 70 yards to start yelling at you," Garrity says. "He'd say, 'Your dad was always better than you! He never would have dropped that!' It worked. It got me so ticked off that I said, 'When I leave here, I want him to say that I was better than my dad.'"

Paterno's prodding paid off. On New Year's Day 1983, Garrity caught the pass that forever made him a legend in Nittany Lion lore.

The Game of My Life
By Gregg Garrity

THE SUGAR BOWL
PENN STATE VERSUS GEORGIA
JANUARY 1, 1983

When I first found out we'd be playing for the national championship, I sat and thought, "God, what a long road." Coming up as a walk-on and now getting a chance to be part of the first team ever from Penn State to win a national title. I thought of all those great teams, and I felt really fortunate.

This was the second year in a row we were going against a Heisman Trophy-winning running back (USC's Marcus Allen won the award in 1981), and Herschel Walker was the big talk. But offensively, we had to deal with Georgia's defensive backs and linebackers, so we had to know more about them than Herschel.

They had Terry Hoag, an All-American safety. He wasn't real fast, but he was smart and a great tackler. They also had a true freshman named Tony Flack. He was spouting off about how good he was and how he was gonna take care of us. I said, "Man, we gotta get this guy." And that was the guy I eventually beat on the touchdown pass.

Joe really kept on us in practice before the game. Throughout that season, we'd only practiced in pads one day a week: Bloody Tuesdays. But before the Sugar Bowl, we practiced in pads a lot more than we were used to. Those first couple weeks were pretty physical; he wanted to make sure we were ready.

We threw a couple wrinkles into the game plan, but nothing major. We were gonna stick with the things that got us there. I think Georgia thought we'd go back to the traditional style of Penn State— just running the ball. But we could do either. If the running game wasn't working, we could start passing, and vice versa. Early on we were doing just that. I had a couple catches, including a crossing route. Another one I caught, but as soon as I hit the ground, it squirted out and was incomplete.

We built a 20-3 lead, but they had experience on us. They'd won a national title [in the 1981 season], and anytime you play an elite school like Georgia, they never quit. That's what makes them good. So when they scored right before halftime, I think it might have even helped. We knew we couldn't just sit back.

When they made it 20-17, it got us back on our heels a little bit. But we knew if we had to score, we could score. I don't think there was any urgency. It was just a matter of let's keep things going.

The play was called "648." Basically, the two outside guys, Kenny Jackson and I, ran "nine routes" or "fly routes." The tight end and [running back] Curt Warner ran seam route nine routes. All four of us were doing the same thing. We ran it all year but I never got it. [Quarterback Todd Blackledge] would always throw it to someone else.

This time when they lined up on defense, I knew I was gonna be open. It was a two-deep zone, so if I beat the cornerback, then the safeties would be occupied by the seam routes. So I just took it. Ran it the same way I ran it all year.

It was perfect. He threw it and I'm watching it the whole way, and I'm thinking, "Come on, come on, come on. Get here faster." It seemed like everything was in slow motion. I said [to myself], "Just catch the ball. Don't drop it." I laid out for it. It wasn't the toughest catch I ever made, but it was pretty tough.

After the score, my first thought was, we needed it. Then I looked at the clock. There was way too much time left. Too much time to relax. It wasn't 'til later in the fourth when I had a catch for a first down that I knew we'd made things real difficult on them. It was only a 7-yard gain, but Joe later said it was just as important as the touchdown catch.

After the game, everyone was going nuts. Watch the attempt at carrying Joe. No one really knew how to do it. Usually they get [the coach] up on shoulders and he is sitting up. Joe was kind of laying with his feet sticking up.

What happened next was even funnier. Todd and Curt [Warner] and I went to do the media thing. It took a while cause they were asking a million questions. When we got back to the locker room, everyone was gone. Everyone. We had no ride. They left us there!

So we showered, put our uniforms in bags and left them there. Todd had the MVP trophy. We went outside and started hitchhiking. We were thumbin'! We saw these people with a van; I think they were with the Audubon Society or something. They said, "Hey, weren't you guys playing?" We're like, "Yeah, they left us here." So they gave us a ride back to the hotel. You think about it now, it's pretty funny. But we were pretty scared. We were like 15, 20 minutes from the hotel. How in the heck were we gonna get back?

At the hotel, the fans were going nuts. It took us almost as long to get through the lobby as it did to get back from the stadium. Finally hotel security got us to the service elevator, and we rode up to the team party, which was in full swing by the time we got there. That was a good time.

Game Results

Penn State was a clear underdog in the sixth postseason matchup between the Associated Press' Nos. 1 and 2 teams since the advent of the AP poll in 1936. Much of that had to do with Heisman Trophy-winning junior Herschel Walker. In 35 games the running back had played at Georgia, the Bulldogs were 33-2.

But Paterno had his troops prepared. Defensively, the "Magic Defense"—"It's called magic," said defensive coordinator Jerry Sandusky, "because sometimes it is. Then again, sometimes it's not"—employed shifting fronts and configurations to confuse Georgia's blockers. PSU tacklers kept Walker moving laterally instead of north-south to allow linebackers and safeties time to finish off what linemen Walker Lee Ashley and Greg Gattuso often started.

Offensively, Blackledge carved up a Dawgs secondary that had intercepted a nation's-best 35 passes coming into the contest. He went 9 of 16 for 160 yards, setting up two Warner touchdown runs and two Nick Gancitano field goals for a 20-3 State lead.

Georgia, though, made it a game. A Herman Archie touchdown grab just before halftime cut it to 20-10, and in the third, Walker plunged in from a yard out to make it 20-17. That's when Garrity hip-faked Flack and burned down the sideline. "I pretty much just threw the ball as far as I could," Blackledge said. Forty-seven famous yards later, Garrity made a lunging grab at the goal line, landed in the end zone, and it was 27-17.

The Dawgs inched as close as 27-23 on a John Lastinger-to-Clarence Kay hookup with 3:54 left in the game. But Walker was stuffed on the ensuing two-point try, and Penn State ran out the clock.

"I kind of felt it would happen," Paterno said afterwards. "I hope nobody doubts we're No. 1 after today. ... This is the best football team I've ever had."

Reflecting on State

Garrity still has his Penn State jersey and helmet. He has other trophies from his days at North Allegheny and his seven NFL seasons—one and a half with the Steelers, five and a half with the Eagles. But if there's anything he treasures most, it's the good fortune that landed him at Penn State and put him in position to make a catch that he says spurred his pro career.

"As you get older, you think about it," says Garrity, now a father of two who lives a quarter-mile from where he grew up in Bradford Woods. "I couldn't have written a better script. Even if you have all the talent in the world, you've got to be a little lucky to get through some things. If you had asked me, 'What would have been your dream final game at Penn State?' That would have been it."

And fans remember. Even now, Garrity, who does renovations and additions with his small firm, All Hands On Deck, still receives copies monthly in the mail of the January 10, 1983, *Sports Illustrated* pronouncing Penn State "No. 1 At Last!" As he did for wide-eyed frat brothers more than 20 years ago, he still signs every issue he receives.

"I thought I'd signed every copy of *SI* out there," he says. "It's unbelievable."

Just like his story.

13

SHANE CONLAN

NAME: Shane Patrick Conlan
BORN: March 4, 1964, in Olean, New York
HOMETOWN: Frewsburg, New York
CURRENT RESIDENCE: Sewickley, Pennsylvania
OCCUPATION: Assistant to NFL agent; former NFL player
POSITION: Outside linebacker
HEIGHT: 6 feet, 3 inches
PLAYING WEIGHT: 230 pounds
YEARS LETTERED: 1983 to 1986
NUMBER WORN AT PSU: 31
ACCOMPLISHMENTS: Sixth-ever two-time All-American at Penn
    State (1985-86) led '86 national championship squad in
    tackles with 79, including team-high 63 solo stops; finished
    career with 274 tackles, fourth all-time in school history; 186
    career solo stops remains school record; first-round draft pick
    of the Buffalo Bills in 1987 won that season's NFL Defensive
    Rookie of the Year honors; played nine NFL seasons with Bills
    and Los Angeles/St. Louis Rams, making three career Pro
    Bowls; member of Buffalo Sports Hall of Fame.
THE GAME: The Fiesta Bowl, Penn State versus Miami,
    January 2, 1987

The Young Life of Shane Conlan

Shane Conlan chuckles at the irony of the situation. He's more than a decade removed from his last NFL game, nearly 20 years since his defensive heroics helped Penn State pluck one of the greatest upsets in college football history. And yet here he is, still limping subtly from the effects of 120 NFL games, and trying to convince oldest son Patrick and Patrick's junior high football teammates not to be like their famous coach.

"I was aggressive, but I was also mean, dirty," says the former two-time Penn State All-American. "I mean, I can't imagine the stuff I used to do. And I'm yelling at these kids for doing the same stuff. I was twice as bad."

He's as nice a guy as you'll meet on a football sideline or golf course—along with coaching, golfing is one of his part-time hobbies these days—but you don't go from small-town unknown to three-time Pro Bowler on the strength of manners between the hashes. Conlan may not have been born with the frame of a hulking footballer, but man, whatever he had beneath those pads, he never feared flinging it into traffic to clog a hole or smack a tailback. "The only regret I had," he says, "and I'm trying to teach my son this, is that sometimes you can avoid blockers rather than trying to go through them."

Try telling that to Shane Conlan circa 1982. That kid was one of the biggest players on the 1981 Frewsberg (N.Y.) Central High football team at all of 6 feet, 2 inches, and 180 pounds. He was also much like his hometown: decent, honest, blue-collar. The *Los Angeles Times* once described Frewsburg, just south of Jamestown near the Pennsylvania border, as having a "wholesome, gutsy bite to it," and anyone who ever saw Conlan blow up an off-tackle run understood the comparison.

One of four kids raised by Kay and Dan, a former investigator for the New York State Police, Shane developed his passion for athletics and his aggressiveness from playing pickup football and baseball with older brother Kevin. The boys were just a year apart, so it was no surprise they competed against each other for Conlan family sports supremacy. "It always ended in a fight," Shane says. "The neighbor

Two-time All-American Shane Conlan played the game with a passion and tenaciousness that embodied the 1986 defense, which he led to Penn State's national championship game upset of Miami. Conlan had eight tackles and two interceptions in a Fiesta Bowl instant classic.

kids would break us up, [then] my mother would come out and send us in."

Shane was a Little League catcher first, since Dan wouldn't let him play football until seventh grade, and then it was only a five-on-five league. Shane's first 11-man football experience was at Frewsburg Central, where he played tailback and linebacker, helping the Bears reach the Section 6 Football Federation playoffs his senior year. Frewsburg was throttled 49-14 by Albion at Rich Stadium, home to Shane's boyhood rooting interest, the Buffalo Bills.

Those playoffs didn't help Conlan's prospect value. He'd scheduled recruiting visits with several schools, Ohio State and Syracuse among them, but every suitor cancelled. Except one: "Penn State," he says calmly, "was the only one that offered me a scholarship."

The Setting

Could Conlan hang at Penn State? He answers one way, then alters his stance. "I knew it would be tough," he says first. "Please, I was the biggest kid on my team at 180 pounds. We were a real small school. Quite frankly, I wasn't sure I could hack it at that level." Then, without much pause, he rebuts himself. "I thought I'd be all right," he says. "My father said I'd be all right. He's like, 'You're gonna do just fine.' But I had no idea. I had never seen kids that big."

Credit Penn State's cafeteria chicken sandwiches or a tested weight program, but either way, within 12 months of Conlan's arrival in Happy Valley, he'd gone from 183 to 210 pounds. By '84 he'd reached 220 pounds.

The skills, plus a stick-his-nose-in-any-scrum moxie, were already obvious. Maturity and technique, he says, were somewhat lacking, and Conlan was redshirted in 1982, spending his first college fall on the scout team. "We were just battering rams," he says of practicing against the 1982 first-team offense.

A year of learning from certain influential teammates (Walker Lee Ashley) and coaches (defensive coordinator Jerry Sandusky) helped Conlan with technique—little things, like how to position his arms, elbows in, thumbs up, so as to best shock and repel would-be blockers with a quick blow. The maturity bit took more time.

"I used to be a jackass," he says, berating himself while masking a smile. "Like I remember on kickoff team my sophomore year—I got in trouble with Joe [Paterno]—I'd run down, you know, covering a kick. Ball's kicked in the end zone, the back line has their backs turned to watch the ball, and I'd just go and run 'em. Hit 'em right in the back."

Fifteen-yard personal foul? "Oh yeah," he adds, "I got a lot of 'em. A *whole* lot of 'em."

There's a twinge of regret tied to this particular tale, but there's also a sense that it's what made Shane Conlan, Shane Conlan. He was young, but he was hungry. "I always had the aggressiveness in me," he says. It showed when he began seeing more regular playing time as a redshirt sophomore in 1984 and redshirt junior in '85, the latter in which he led 11-1 Penn State in solo tackles (57), finishing third in total tackles (91). The Nittany Lions fell to Oklahoma in the Orange Bowl that season, after which Conlan could have departed Penn State in the 1986 NFL draft.

Like so many before and since, Conlan went to Paterno for advice. But unlike so many before and since, Conlan decided beforehand that he would actually base his decision on Paterno's opinion. When Paterno's league sources came back with reports that Conlan would likely go between the second and fourth rounds, the linebacker didn't balk, deciding on the spot to return for his senior season.

Conlan can't recall for sure if Paterno had anything to do with it (he suspects as much), but before playing a down in '86, the fifth-year senior and his father took out a Lloyd's of London insurance policy in the event he got hurt that season. Dan Conlan never told Shane the value of the policy opened for his son (estimates placed it between $500,000 and $1 million). Besides, Shane had bigger things to think about, like helping the Lions find their way back to the national title game, a journey that culminated in the Arizona desert on the second night of 1987.

The Game of My Life
By Shane Conlan

THE FIESTA BOWL
PENN STATE VERSUS MIAMI
JANUARY 2, 1987

To get that far two years in a row is pretty unheard of. I mean, most teams usually get there once. It's like playing in a Super Bowl. You never know when you're gonna get back there. So we knew it would be a tough road. But I knew we'd be good, especially defensively.

The way Joe would build a team was defense one, offense two. That year we had two of the best backs in the country. Blair Thomas was just unbelievable, and D.J. Dozier was a first-round draft choice. On defense we were a really tight group of guys. For the most part, we all came in together and all got redshirted together, so we pretty much matured together as players.

At linebacker we had Trey Bauer, who was just a mouth. He wasn't the cleanest player on the team either, so he and I used to fight over who got the most personal fouls. Then Donnie Graham, a great athlete and great pass rusher. Pete Giftopolous was always around the ball. He made so many big plays. We had good defensive linemen, great nose tackles. I know I got a lot of the publicity, but it doesn't work without 11 guys.

I remember going to all those All-American things between the end of the season and the bowl, and seeing all those guys from Miami. Vinny Testaverde, Jerome Brown, Alonzo Highsmith. They were like, "We want to stay." They wanted to stay home and play in the Orange Bowl. You gotta be kidding me. Obviously somebody got to them, cause they came to Tempe and played us. And we loved it. We wanted to play the No. 1 team. Back then they could have chosen not to play us, and we would have had no shot. So obviously we owe them a lot, cause they didn't have to play us.

I remember how funny it was when they walked out. (Miami players shocked bowl organizers by walking out of a planned bowl week steak fry.) Like that really bothered us. It's not like we were talking to them anyway. I just think it was bad for the bowl people. They went to a lot of trouble putting that thing together. Then they just got up and walked out. I know for a fact, no Joe Paterno-coached team would have ever walked out of there. They'd be on the next plane ride home if they tried to pull that. So from that sense it was good. And it was good in the media. They pitted good versus evil, which was kind of cool.

Early on we went to this different kind of defense [called] "The Bubble." They actually had put it in the year before, but we hadn't used it much. I kind of just floated around and read the quarterback. And it was more than just individual efforts. You needed to have everybody flying to the ball.

Many times before the game, Jerry [Sandusky] had said, "You can't stop every play from happening. You just gotta minimize it." So we knew we weren't going to shut 'em down. Still, I think we really lucked out with Testaverde not having a great game. If he was on, who knows? I don't think it would have gone as well. And we were surprised. I mean, a couple of those throws, I don't know if they were bad reads or poor throws or what. He hit me in the face with one.

Still, we knew they were gonna catch the ball. It was just how hard could we get 'em down. When you hit a guy in the mouth, whew. That affects people. It really does. You don't know if they're gonna go up and get it next time. I remember one hit [PSU safety] Ray Isom put on [Miami wideout] Michael Irvin. That was pretty good. I was right there yelling something at Irvin, and I'm pretty sure it wasn't very nice.

I remember my interception in the fourth. We were in that Bubble defense. I was floating around and read the quarterback. I jumped and caught it. I thought I made a pretty good catch. To this day my brothers still think I should have scored. "Why couldn't you jump over him?" I jumped and just flopped. I don't know. I must have been really tired.

After we scored to take the lead, we knew they weren't gonna get a whole lot. But unfortunately they went right down the field. You're talking about one of the most prolific passing teams of that year, maybe ever. It was just a matter of time before they were gonna complete some passes. But you've got to hang in there. Bend a little, bend a little, then maybe something good will happen, which it obviously did.

I was on the other side of the field, just dropping. Then I looked and I just couldn't understand who Testaverde was throwing it to. There were like three guys there, and they were all us. I think if Pete [Giftopolous] didn't have [the interception], Donnie Graham did. I don't know if he tried to force it or what, but he threw it right to him.

It was a long time ago, but I remember the excitement. On the other hand, we were so tired. I remember right after the game, Ahmad Rashad grabbed me right next to Joe. The whole thing was surreal. They stick a mic in and interview you and it's like wow, kind of cool.

Afterwards I was one of the last guys out of the locker room. And Vinny Testaverde came over into our locker room and congratulated us—congratulated me. I thought that was awesome. He came up, sought me out, we talked, and it was good. That was really a class thing for him to do.

Game Results

Conlan had first met Testaverde more than a year before the Fiesta Bowl, and by the time Penn State and Miami met for the national championship, the two called each other friends. Conlan recounts the story of traveling to a postseason event in December 1986, just after Testaverde had won the Heisman. When the Miami quarterback, flying first class, learned Conlan was onboard and flying in the back of the plane, he had a flight attendant move Conlan's seat next to his in first class.

Still, in the buildup to the battle of No. 1 Miami vs. No. 2 Penn State, Conlan had no trouble broadcasting his intentions come kickoff. "I'm still going to hit him," Conlan said. "I don't care whether he's a friend. I want to hit him as hard as I can. I want to hit everybody as hard as I can. I don't care if it's my mother or my brother."

It was vintage Conlan, as was State's defensive performance in the Fiesta Bowl. What made it sweeter for the Lions was how much talking the talented, healthily confident Hurricanes had done leading into the game. The Canes, who'd arrived in Arizona wearing Army fatigues and had worn sweats and T's to one pre-bowl luncheon, swore at Penn State players and coaches during pregame warmups. The 6-foot, 2-inch Irvin laughed in the shorter Isom's face. "You're Isom?" he asked. "Oh *man*." Said Miami's Alonzo Highsmith to Penn State's Duffy Cobbs, "You shouldn't have come, you know. It's too late to turn back. You've chosen your own death now."

It all served as inspiration for Penn State. Before 73,098 fans and 70 million TV viewers—it remains the most-watched college football game of all time—Penn State played four quarters of inspired bend-don't-break football.

Miami struck first, scoring four plays after forcing Penn State quarterback John Shaffer to fumble deep in PSU territory. Shaffer answered, though, leading the conservative Penn State offense on its only true sustained drive of the day. The quarterback scored on a 4-yard scramble to cap a 13-play, 74-yard drive. The score was knotted, 7-7, at halftime.

After a scoreless third, Miami regained the lead on Mark Seelig's 38-yard field goal. But with 8:13 remaining in the game, Conlan picked off his second pass—he'd also killed a Canes drive late in the third by intercepting Testaverde at Penn State's 17—and returned it 39 yards to Miami's 6. Two plays later, D.J. Dozier slipped into the end zone, then kneeled to pray. Penn State led 14-10.

Miami's final chance came with less than four minutes remaining. After converting a clutch fourth-and-6 at his own 27, Testaverde completed four more passes in a row, the last three to Irvin. Miami reached Penn State's 6-yard-line on fourth down with nine seconds remaining. Testaverde, hoping to hit Brett Perriman on a curl, instead saw his 50th and final attempt of the night nestle into the waiting arms of State's Giftopolous. It was Testaverde's fifth interception of the night, hard to believe considering he'd gone 114 passes without a pick earlier in the season.

"I think we played the game the way we wanted to play it," said Paterno of winning despite Miami's 93 plays and 445 yards of total offense to Penn State's 59 plays for 162 yards. "Be patient. They're going to make yardage. You're out there to win a football game, not to see how many stats you can get. I'm not going to let a bunch of statistics change the score."

"Wouldn't it have been a shame if we hadn't played this game?" Paterno added. "If we had not had a shot at them, Miami would have been voted No. 1, no question. Instead, we got to find out who was better."

In finishing 12-0 and handing Paterno his second national title in five years, the Lions pulled off one of the greatest upsets in college football history. Conlan won outstanding defensive player honors for his eight tackles and two picks, yet he credited State's short yet stout secondary for setting the tone. "Those little guys just rocked 'em," he said, "and they didn't want to catch the ball anymore."

Reflecting on State

Despite holding out of camp in a contract dispute and moving from outside to inside linebacker when Buffalo acquired Cornelius Bennett at midseason, Conlan's talents shined through in 1987, his NFL rookie year. He led the team in tackles with 114, 33 more than Buffalo's second-leading tackler. He went on to play in three Super Bowls with the Bills in 1991, '92, and '93, losing all three times, before signing as a free agent with the Rams, with whom he played his final three seasons in the league.

Those Super Bowl losses still sting, but they also help Conlan continually cherish the magnitude of winning what he says was the biggest game he ever played in. "I just think of the defensive effort," he says of the Fiesta Bowl. "Defensively we won another game for Penn State, which I take a lot of pride in."

He's still close with many teammates from that '86 roster, guys like defensive ends Bob White and Dan Delligatti, safety Mike Zordich (a current golfing buddy), and Chris Collins, an ex-special teams captain and Conlan's college roommate who was also a member of his wedding party.

Conlan gets to one or two games a season these days, one with his pals, one with his family. He and wife Carolyn, a Penn Stater as well, have four children: Patrick, his oldest, followed by Christopher, Mary

Katherine, and Daniel. He sells a little life insurance locally near his home in Sewickley, Pennsylvania, and assists his former agent, Brett Senior, in landing new clients, former Nittany Lions included. (Conlan helped Senior sign Zack Mills and Andrew Guman in 2004.)

Conlan speaks quickly and directly, and he's not much for glory stories. His preferred personal legacy? "A nice, tough kid," he says. "I didn't celebrate a whole lot. Just a quiet kid who played hard."

And the '86 team's legacy? "I think it probably goes down as the biggest underdog in history to win a game," he says as the game's 20-year anniversary approaches. "You just know good defense can carry you."

That sentiment never gets old in Happy Valley.

14

CRAIG FAYAK

NAME: Craig Michael Fayak
BORN: July 22, 1972, in Charleroi, Pennsylvania
HOMETOWN: Belle Vernon, Pennsylvania
CURRENT RESIDENCE: New York City, New York
OCCUPATION: Vice president of sales operations, PDI, Inc.
POSITION: Placekicker
HEIGHT: 6 feet, 2 inches
PLAYING WEIGHT: 175 pounds
YEARS LETTERED: 1990 to 1993
NUMBER WORN AT PSU: 5
ACCOMPLISHMENTS: Led Penn State in scoring in 1990, '91
    and '93 seasons, and remains State's all-time scoring leader
    with 282 points; his 50 field goals and 80 FG attempts are
    also school career records; hit a Lions-record 13 straight field
    goals in 1992; first-team Academic All-American in 1993 is
    one of only 18 Nittany Lion football players ever to receive an
    NCAA postgraduate scholarship.
THE GAME: Penn State at Notre Dame, November 17, 1990

The Young Life of Craig Fayak

Pick an afternoon in 1988 or '89, and chances are Craig Fayak was in his backyard teeing up footballs, pacing off steps, ripping into the pigskins with his whiplash right leg, and watching kicks sail through his father's homemade goalpost. The regularity of Fayak's kicking sessions may have varied by season—daily practice in summer and fall, weekend practice when basketball and baseball schedules limited his free time in winter and spring. But his routine never wavered: a brief warmup, then sets of five boots from specifically targeted spots, followed by scattered kicks from mixed distances and angles. Finally, just before heading inside, he'd allow himself to daydream a little.

"It was always a field goal to beat Notre Dame, to beat USC, to beat Alabama," says Fayak, whose boyhood kicks of faux glory would become reality in 1990, hundreds of miles away in northern Indiana. "I would end every practice with a shot. And I wouldn't kick another one. If I missed it, I was done. I didn't miss very often."

Fayak's father, Jack, a steel mill worker in Pittsburgh, had built the family goalpost in the early 1980s for Craig's older brother, Jack Jr., to use for target practice. But when Jack Jr., Craig's elder by six years, left home in 1985 to kick at West Virginia's Bethany College, the backyard uprights were all Craig's. "I would practice almost every single day," he says. "And I loved it too, so it wasn't really work."

There often isn't a ton of demand for kickers out of high school, especially at the Division I-A level. As a senior at Belle Vernon (Pennsylvania) High, Fayak's best option in the fall of 1989 looked like a baseball scholarship to either Oklahoma or William & Mary. Football recruiters wanted him to walk on. West Virginia flat ignored him. Pitt never once spoke to him. Then Jerry Sandusky got involved.

The Penn State defensive coordinator began courting Fayak as purely an athlete, his position to be determined later. Fayak visited University Park, met fellow high school seniors like Kerry Collins and Kyle Brady and fell in love with Joe Paterno's "Do it my way or don't bother" mantra. "He said, 'You have to go to class, you have to stay out of trouble and you need to practice hard,'" Fayak recalls of

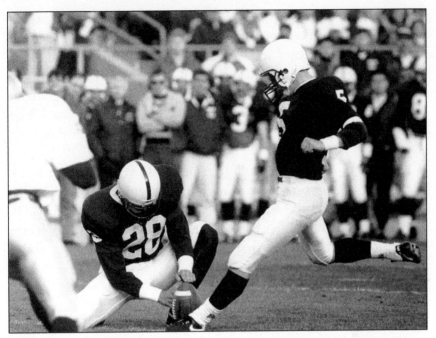

Craig Fayak's 34-yard field goal was the game winner in Penn State's 1990 upset of Notre Dame in South Bend, Indiana. The former Academic All-American remains State's all-time scoring leader.

Paterno's message. "'Then we might consider giving you some playing time.' God, I loved that. It was me."

The Setting

Fayak's opportunities to contribute in 1990 seemed limited, especially considering Paterno's penchant for rewarding the commitment of upperclassmen. Henry Adkins, a senior who'd bided his time behind Ray Tarasi, was named starter for State's 1990 opener against Texas at Beaver Stadium. V.J. Muscillo, a high-school All-American who redshirted in '89, waited in the wings. But Paterno and the coaching staff immediately recognized the kid from Belle Vernon's leg strength, and they opted not to redshirt him. In fact, they gave Fayak kickoff duties against the Longhorns. Then it all happened:

Adkins blew a pair of field goals in the Lions' 17-13 loss, by which time Muscillo had been converted to a punter.

"The next Monday I walked into practice," Fayak says, "and one of the coaches pulled me aside and said, 'Son, this is gonna be a big week in your life.' I didn't know what he meant. I remember going to my locker and opening up my little cubbyhole, and there was a blue jersey there, which means you're first team. They gave me a shot right away."

Just weeks into his first college semester, 18-year-old Craig Fayak boarded a plane for California to start his first game in blue and white. "I was scared to death," he says of Penn State's September 15, 1990, road game at USC. "Especially at that age, there's so much change going on anyway. You're leaving home for the first time, going to this big university, and meeting new people. Now you're thrown into situations right away where there's 90,000 people and television cameras everywhere. You're also struggling with the fact that this is something you've always dreamed of."

The dream was too good to be true, and Fayak watched it first-hand: The Trojans streaming onto the field; ABC television crews; painted faces; the USC band and equine mascot, Traveler; the Goodyear blimp; his first field goal attempt as a Nittany Lion, from 39 yards out, sailing wide left. "I pulled it," he says. "It was the worst, disgusting feeling. I'd never felt so sick in my life."

Penn State lost, 19-14, and flew back to Pennsylvania with an 0-2 record. Though the Lions blanked Rutgers 28-0 the following week at home, Fayak had his lone field goal try blocked by the Scarlet Knights, shuttling him into an off week with brittle confidence and an ugly O-fer in the field goal column. An uncomfortable two weeks later, Fayak found himself still wearing the blue jersey for Game 4 against Temple. In the waning moments of the first half, he drilled a 45-yarder, then knocked home another in the second half. Penn State 48, Temple 10. The ensuing Saturday, State's third consecutive home game, Fayak's two field goals were the difference in a 27-21 defeat of Syracuse. The roll, as it goes, was on.

"Confidence for an athlete is a funny thing," Fayak says. "You don't know how you get it or lose it. But you know when you have it." He had it on October 27, drilling three more field goals in a 9-0 win at Alabama. For the acutely focused frosh, that was a defining moment. He recognized that he indeed was Penn State's first-string kicker and a calm, consistent specialist whom teammates could lean on and coaches could leave alone.

That was key when Penn State traveled to South Bend for a November 17 showdown. Notre Dame had it all clicking: a No. 1 Associated Press ranking; so much history; those darn echoes; and a four-pack of All-Americans, none more capable of instantly altering a game than shifty flanker-tailback Raghib "Rocket" Ismail. Plus, when Penn State came calling, the Fighting Irish also had a national championship in their sights and a boisterous 59,075 on hand to remind them of their destiny. Across the grass stood the Nittany Lions, a bunch that had lost their last two brawls with Notre Dame. Of course, since starting 0-2, State had won seven straight to crawl back into the Top 25.

As State streaked, Fayak blossomed. In practice before the showdown with the Irish, the kicker noticed a quiet confidence about his teammates, a harnessed excitement that they might do something shocking in South Bend. Fayak slept well the night of Thursday, November 15, awaking to sharp recollections of a dream. He had to spill the details, and roommate Kyle Brady, a redshirt tight end, was in the room.

"This is a true story," Fayak begins. "I told Kyle before we left, 'I had a dream last night. I don't know if it's just wishful thinking, but I had a dream that I'm gonna kick a field goal and we're gonna beat this team.' I remember at the time the newspapers quoted it also, cause I said truly, I swear, 'I just had a dream I was gonna kick a field goal to beat Notre Dame.' It was the Friday before we flew out."

The Game of My Life
By Craig Fayak

PENN STATE AT NOTRE DAME
NOVEMBER 17, 1990

I remember Joe gave a speech the night before the game. He said, "You know, the Four Horsemen aren't going to show up. Knute Rockne's not gonna be there. The ghosts aren't going to be there. It's a 100-yard field…" You wanted to go out and play that night. It got everybody so focused on what we had an opportunity to do. It was just a great speech. I'll never forget it.

On game day, I remember going into the locker room. The visitors locker room was really dark, really small, really dingy—probably by design. It almost felt like a high school locker room. I remember going out on the field for pregame. It was a 4:30 start, so the sun was setting. It was November, chilly. The field was pretty beat up and the grass was pretty tall, too. I was surprised, but none of that mattered because you were at Notre Dame. The stadium had so much history and it was a neat feeling to play a team like that. Then again, we had that tradition also. You sensed something special was going to happen.

They handled us pretty well in the first half. We were losing 21-7, and no one was excited. At halftime Joe said, "Look, they've played about as well as they can play. We've played about as poorly as we can play. They're up two touchdowns. Everyone hang in there and we're gonna win this game."

We started to drive right in the beginning of the second half, but I missed a field goal, a 39-yarder. I missed it about half a foot to the right. I was so demoralized. There are certain field goals a kicker can miss and get away with. There are others you just have to have. That was one of them. I was so disgusted that I remembered saying, "I just want to walk off this field right now."

Then they got the ball and threw an interception right away to Mark D'Onofrio. Then Tony Sacca threw the third-down pass to [wideout] Ricky Sayles on an option route. We were right back in it. I remember us getting the ball back and Sacca rolling out and throwing a curlback pass to [tight end] Al Golden and Al going in. The extra point happened so fast, I didn't even think about it. I just felt momentum was on our side. There were probably six or seven minutes left in the game. All I could do was wait and see what happened.

When Darren Perry intercepted that pass, I remember my knees sort of buckling a little bit. It's hard to describe the amount of weight you feel on your shoulders. While you're looking forward to going out there, you start having crazy thoughts like, "If I left right now, if I ran through the tunnel, would anyone know?" You start to realize the only way you're going to get into that tunnel and on a plane home is after these next 25 or 30 minutes of your life.

I remember Sam Gash came over to me and started to say something, and I literally went like this (extends hands in a stopping motion) and said, "Sam, get away from me. Let me do my thing." That's about the only moment I could push Sam Gash away.

I remember I felt comfortable. I still see the goalposts. I still see the darkness behind it. I can see the little clump of grass that was almost like a tee—a nice high spot. It was really perfect how it all laid out: Bill Spoor was the holder. He had such a commanding, quiet confidence that was so needed for a freshman like myself. Bob Ceh was the snapper. He had started off as one of our equipment managers. About the second game of the year, our long snapper got in trouble with Joe and Joe benched him. We didn't have a snapper. Bob said, "I did it in high school. I can snap." He was amazing.

Bob's snap wasn't perfect, but it was a good snap. Bill picked it up like he did a million times. As soon as I hit it, I knew. When the ball went through, it went silent. There's something very empowering about making that crowd go silent. Cause you know if you'd missed it, they'd have gone crazy. It was a neat moment.

Afterwards, the locker room was bedlam. I remember seeing Jim Caldwell, our quarterbacks coach. I'll never forget the look on his face.

Guys are congratulating each other, hugging each other, and he just kind of stopped and looked at me. He had this look like, "Son, you have no idea how your life just changed." I'll never forget that look. Then he gave me a hug and we went on celebrating.

Game Results

No. 18 Penn State's upset of top-ranked and seven-point-favorite Notre Dame—the fifth time that season a No. 1-ranked squad had lost—was clearly a tale of two halves. In the first, ND running backs Ricky Watters and Tony Brooks each averaged 6-plus yards per carry, and Ismail collected 98 all-purpose yards to help the Irish amass 292 yards of total offense. They scored on three of their five possessions, and the other two trips, kicker Craig Hentrich missed field goals of 43 and 53 yards.

Down 21-7 at the half, Paterno asked more of his troops. "We weren't aggressive enough," he said. "I felt we were giving too much respect to their receivers. I said, 'Go out there, take a chance, make something happen.'"

It didn't hurt that before the end of the first half, the speedy Ismail had aggravated a badly bruised right thigh. Rocket never returned to the game in the second. Without his game-breaker, Irish sophomore quarterback Rick Mirer struggled. After Fayak missed his 39-yard field goal, D'Onofrio picked off Mirer's throw near midfield and returned it to the Irish 11. Three plays later Sacca found wide receiver Sayles to bring the Lions within one score, 21-14.

In the fourth, a missed tackle by Notre Dame All-American Todd Lyght allowed State wideout Terry Smith to sprint 24 yards to the Irish 34. Moments later, Sacca, a junior who had been pulled several times in previous games for his inconsistency, hit Golden from 14 yards out to tie the score. Sacca would finish 20 of 34 for a career-high 277 yards and three touchdowns.

Still, the defense deserved the largest chunk of credit. After a spotty first half, the Nittany Lions dominated the line of scrimmage and held Notre Dame to 75 yards in the second half. ND's eight second-half possessions netted zero points, and the Irish never crossed midfield after halftime. When Mirer—he entered the game having tossed four interceptions all season—threw his second pick of the night, to Darren Perry in Irish territory with 59 ticks left, the scene was set for Fayak. Paterno's offense ran the clock down to eight seconds and called timeout, after which the freshman calmly connected from 34 yards, sending blue and white believers—a small contingent in the stands and thousands more watching on ESPN—into a frenzy over the 24-21 Penn State victory.

Notre Dame closed its locker room to media after the loss; its national title hopes were dead. Meanwhile, back in State College, hundreds of hyper students clogged College Avenue, rocking cars and honking horns. Some bee-lined for Beaver Stadium, only to find security officers blocking the gates.

On the field, Penn State won out the regular season before falling 24-17 to Florida State in the Blockbuster Bowl for a 9-3 finish. Fayak was bathed in unthinkable glory after his heroic boot in South Bend, but his best friends like Brady sensed the best had come and gone. "Kyle used to joke with me, 'Oh, that was it. You're done, it doesn't get any better.'" Fayak says. "Turns out, it really was. It was the only last-second kick I ever had."

Reflecting on State

Fayak's career didn't end after November 17, 1990. In fact, he kicked three more seasons for Paterno, none more difficult than his junior year. He hurt himself lifting and training for the 1992 campaign, but the extent of the injury was not known until the sixth game that year, when he had a field goal blocked and also missed a 20-yard chip shot in a 17-14 loss at No. 2-ranked Miami. Turns out he had a stress fracture in a back vertebrae, a pain he recalls today being "like a knife shoved in your back."

"As high as the Notre Dame game was," he says, "[Miami] was the lowest of all possible lows." Exacerbating the pain was fear he might never kick again, not to mention death threats he began receiving from maniacal State fans. "I probably should have taken them more seriously than I did, but what are you gonna do?" he says. "You learn a lot about yourself when you go through the highest and lowest moments. You become a man. That's when you grow up.

"To this day, it gives me a tremendous amount of confidence [to know that] I've been tested under those circumstances. ... I carry it with me wherever I go."

Fayak endured nearly eight months of daily therapy to return for his senior year. In an October 1993 game at Ohio State, he nailed a 49-yarder in mud and snow (a nod to his Belle Vernon backyard beginnings) to vault himself atop Penn State's all-time scoring chart. He signed with the Dallas Cowboys in 1994, but lost the kicking job to Chris Boniol. In the fall of '94, Fayak returned to State College to work with kicker Brett Conway as well as the defensive foreign team for a Nittany Lions squad that won the Rose Bowl.

There were more tryouts—in Jacksonville, Miami, and Indianapolis—but Fayak never won a starting job in the NFL. That dream is now over, though he still tees 'em up every summer to teach kickers at Penn State's summer camp. That's only four hours by car from his home in Manhattan, where he reverse commutes every day to a New Jersey-based contract sales company called PDI, which helps pharmaceutical companies with market research and promoting products to doctors.

On display in his apartment, Fayak still has the game ball from that fateful November day in South Bend, along with a photo of a boyish version of himself, arms raised in triumph after the kick of a lifetime. "That moment was special," he says, "and it's hard for me to describe how much I learned about myself by living it. Being part of something so much bigger than you—the history of Penn State football—is something a lot of people can't say [they've done]. It means a lot to me."

15

BUCKY GREELEY

NAME: Paul "Bucky" Domero Greeley
BORN: July 30, 1972, in Wilkes-Barre, Pennsyvlania
HOMETOWN: Wilkes-Barre, Pennsylvania
CURRENT RESIDENCE: Charlotte, North Carolina
OCCUPATION: Senior sales rep for Novo Nordisk Inc.; former NFL player
POSITION: Center
HEIGHT: 6 feet, 2 ½ inches
PLAYING WEIGHT: 270 pounds
YEARS LETTERED: 1991 to 1994
NUMBER WORN AT PSU: 60
ACCOMPLISHMENTS: Played in 1990 Big 33 All-Star football game; started two games each as redshirt freshman and sophomore at Penn State before becoming full-time starting center his last two seasons; co-captain of 1994 Rose Bowl-champion Nittany Lions, the first 12-0 team in Big Ten history; second-team All-Big Ten pick in 1994 also took that year's Maginnis Award, given to the outstanding Penn State offensive lineman who exemplifies the spirit, dedication and commitment of former Lion Richard Maginnis; free-agent signee played for the Carolina Panthers from 1996 to 1998.
THE GAME: Penn State at Michigan, October 15, 1994

The Young Life of Bucky Greeley

Bucky couldn't take it. He was 12 years old, and yeah, he was supposed to be watching older brother Jerry's baseball game. Penn State was hosting the Keystone Games at its baseball complex, just west of the football stadium, and Jerry had made Pennsylvania's Northeast Region roster. But young Bucky couldn't help it. Beaver Stadium was so close he could touch it, a titanic erector set beckoning for attention. Every inning of Jerry's game Bucky tugged at his father and then his grandfather, saying "It's right *there*. Beaver Stadium! Can we go see it?"

"It looked like possibly the biggest thing on Earth," says Bucky, nicknamed for a childhood resemblance to former New York Yankees shortstop Bucky Dent. "What kind of mass could hold 84,000 people?"

In a lull between baseball games, he found out. The Greeleys walked to the stadium, and, finding an open gate (courtesy of construction workers), they ventured in. Bucky's father, also named Jerry, asked a crewman if his eager son could walk on the field. "I went out and ran around," Bucky says. "From midfield, I could look straight up and still see seats. I was amazed by it. When I came jogging off, I told my father and grandfather, 'I'm gonna play here someday.'"

They laughed. Bucky had never played a down of organized football. Baseball was his family's passion; it's still his favorite sport today. His grandfather was a sandlot whiz in Wilkes-Barre. Brother Jerry, now head baseball coach at King's College in Wilkes-Barre and a minor league coach in the summer, tutored Bucky throughout their boyhood, stealing tips from his games to pass to his younger brother. (There's also a third Greeley boy, D.J., five years younger than Bucky.)

Bucky got a late start on football because it cut into his baseball schedule. And even then, Dad's policy was grades came first. If Bucky earned high marks, he could play baseball. Keep it up, he could go out for wrestling. A few more A's and B's, he could try football.

When he finally experienced football as an eighth-grader playing for his junior high team, he migrated to the position that suited him best: center. A catcher in baseball, he thrived on living at the center of

As co-captain for the 1994 Nittany Lions, Bucky Greeley anchored a dominating offensive line that paved the way for Penn State to roll up an NCAA-best 47.8 points and 520.2 yards per game en route to that season's Rose Bowl victory.

the action, calling plays and leading teammates. Throw in his wrestling abilities—he became Wyoming Valley's top scholastic wrestler his senior year at James M. Coughlin High—and trench life seemed apropos.

Coach John Joseph's Coughlin program was much like Joe Paterno's at Penn State. Pay your dues and you will work your way into meaningful minutes on the field. Greeley was somewhat of an anomaly, starting at center as a sophomore. He played both ways the next two seasons, learning the art of blocking from line coach Andy Kuhl. "He taught me things I used until my last year as a Carolina Panther," Greeley says of Kuhl.

Penn State's Jim Williams (Bucky calls him "Ace," a nickname Williams used) recruited Greeley, and it wasn't a hard sell. Deep down Greeley had always wanted to play at Penn State after watching the Lions on TV for years and jogging on that hallowed turf as a youth. He'd wondered what it might be like to someday play alongside Coughlin High legend Dave Brzenchek, a standout lineman who landed at Penn State in 1986. Greeley took his time examining offers from the likes of USC, Maryland, Virginia, and others, but ultimately he began canceling visits because, he says, "I knew where I wanted to go. I had made my decision and went with it."

The Setting

Greeley arrived at Penn State in 1990 with a recruiting class marked for stardom: Kerry Collins, Kyle Brady, Derek Bochna, Craig Fayak, Brian Gelzheiser—all guys who helped the Pennsylvania All-Stars beat Maryland 42-28 in 1990's Big 33 Game. "You went to Penn State back then to play for a national championship," says Greeley, who as a freshman remembers seeing the 1986 national title rings of the fifth-year seniors, Brzenchek among them. "Anything short of that was unacceptable. I went in there thinking, I hope to God I'm not the class that ends the streak."

Three years later, it looked like his class might be headed in that direction. Talented Nittany Lion squads went 9-3 in 1990 (including a Blockbuster Bowl loss to Florida State) and 11-2 in '91 (capped by a 42-17 Fiesta Bowl thumping of Tennessee). But after a 5-0 start in '92, State dropped five of its last seven for a disappointing 7-5 record. For Greeley it was an eye-opener, "because I didn't go to Penn State to win seven games," he says. "There was a lot of soul searching."

Paterno and staff concluded that by improving internal communication, it would help restore a roster that had lost trust in the assistants' abilities to put players in good situations to win. Paterno hastened change in the spring of 1993 by calling in upperclassmen by position, including offensive linemen Greeley, guard Mike Malinoski, and tackle Derick Pickett. "[Paterno] made it pretty clear that day that if we were gonna get something done, he needed it from us," Greeley says. "And if we were unwilling or unable to do it, we might want to look into another means of paying for our education."

The success of 1994's squad was born within those position meetings. And somewhere between his own one-on-one meeting with Paterno and ensuing regular Tuesday morning breakfasts with the grandfatherly head coach and other teammates, Greeley emerged as a vocal, astute, likeable leader of the Lions. It helped that he knew his history, that he'd learned his trade and the Penn State Way from offensive linemen before him like Brzenchek, Rob Luedeke, Pat Duffy, Todd Rucci, and Matt McCartin. It also helped that Greeley, perhaps more than any player in his recruiting class, could be frank with Paterno on any issue. He was brutally honest about the team's problems in 1992 in their first closed-door talk. Later, in preparation for the 1995 Rose Bowl, he chided Joe about adding patches to those beautifully plain uniforms.

"I said, 'We're getting Big Ten patches and Rose Bowl patches. It's bad enough we have to wear [Nike] swooshes on our uniforms so you and your wife can go on a free cruise every year,'" Greeley says. "He started laughing, but the person who suffered most was Spider Caldwell, our equipment manager. He and his wife had already sewn patches on half the jerseys. Joe went and told him, 'Well, we're not doing the patches.'"

Besides increased communication and trust, Penn State's revival was propelled by experience and trust at its core, the offensive line. In 1992, Greeley, Jeff Hartings, Keith Conlin, Marco Rivera, and Andre

Johnson played much of the season together on second team. They grew tighter in 1993, even though Rivera, Hartings, and Greeley were starters with Malinoski and Pickett. "When I made a certain call, I knew exactly where Hartings or Rivera was going to be," Greeley says. "We knew how each other communicated."

That bond grew with trips to the State College Veterans of Foreign Wars club, where the linemen made regular Thursday trips for $3.99 cheesesteak and fries specials. Eventually, success on the field became linked to VFW pilgrimages. "Before it was all said and done, we had passes," says Greeley, who along with Malinoski, started the tradition in 1993. "We didn't need to knock anymore. We had the card you could slide in, the buzzer rang and we went through."

Of course, before they could devour the 1994 Big Ten schedule, the Lions endured a summer of lifting, sweating, and studying to help them do something special that fall. Part of their drive centered on avenging a '93 loss to Michigan, a game in which the Wolverines stopped Penn State four times in a key goal-line stand. In August 1994, when coaches rolled that tape from '93, the room of Lions went silent.

The Game of My Life
By Bucky Greeley

PENN STATE AT MICHIGAN
OCTOBER 15, 1994

There was a time in my life when I could close my eyes, and before I'd go to sleep, I'd see those plays. When you're thinking about the tradition of Penn State football, and that series against Michigan stood between us and a Big Ten championship, it haunts you. We watched that tape. It was a reminder that [Michigan is] working hard, too. ... We need to figure out a way to work a little harder.

I think the biggest asset that '94 team had was a businesslike approach. Whereas in the past we might have let things like [looking ahead to Michigan] deter us from doing well, we literally took one step at a time. Who's in front of us this week? We have to prepare for it like it's a national championship game. We realized in order to beat Michigan, there were five other teams we had to beat first.

We had an off week before Michigan. I remember coming into game week and going in shoulder pads and helmets on a Tuesday or Wednesday. The old, fabled Bloody Tuesday in Penn State lore. Joe looked at us and said, "You guys know how to hit." He goes, "If you guys don't know how to hit by now, there's nothing we can do for you. We gotta get ready to go play a good team." It was an approach I'd equate to a playoff-bound NFL team.

I remember finishing my Thursday workout. I was the last one in the weight room—nobody else was around. I remember laying there doing my stretching, staring up at the ceiling, looking at the flags for the '82 and '86 national championships, saying to myself, this is it. If the '94 team wants to be remembered, it has to happen Saturday. I can't go, "Well, played 'em tough this year, wait 'til next year when everybody's a year older." No. No more next year for me.

The weather was perfect that day. The fans were perfect. The setting was national TV. If you were a recruiting coordinator for either school, you couldn't draw it up any better. We went up early, and we were accustomed to jumping out on people. But we also knew we were playing in the Big House, and Michigan is not going to lay down. We knew there was going to be a counterpunch.

Late in the game, we finished a play, and one of the Michigan players pushed me in the back as I was walking to the huddle. I turned around, and the guy got defensive, ready to take a punch. I was like, "Don't do that. This has been too good of a game and you have played too hard to ruin it with cheap shots." He's like, "You know what, you're right. Sorry about that." We shook hands and went back to our respective huddles. That's the kind of game it was. You could have had a microphone down on that field and you wouldn't have heard any talk. It was mutual respect, guys hitting each other, helping each other up. There was no smack talk, nothing. It was exactly how a purist would draw up a game.

And it couldn't have been any better than coming down to getting a drive and a play to win the game. I always remember the sense of calm, knowing who we are and what we could do at all times. Here we are, our season in the balance, no penalties, in and out of the huddle, up to the line, pressing the tempo, doing the things that got us there. Breaking Ki-Jana [Carter] for a big run. Protecting Kerry, giving him the time to look off two coverages and find Bobby [Engram]. It was everything we'd prepared for. We had placed an importance on doing the little things correctly, and it built up to where everything fell in place for that game.

When Bobby scored, the silence was deafening. Michigan and its fans have an expectation that they don't lose too often in that stadium. That band, they play "Fight on Blue, Hail to the ..." whatever the heck it is. They're used to that ringing out all game long. But when it came down to it, they're like, "Jeez, we can't stop these guys. Even if we score again, they're probably going to score again."

After winning that game, I'm not afraid to admit it. I cried. Just that relief, knowing what those plays the year before meant to our season. They cost us a championship. Now we were 6-0, and I'd never been 6-0. The self-reflection I had two days prior in the weight room, this was it. We did it.

Game Results

For two straight years, Penn State's 5-0 starts had been derailed in Game 6. In 1993 against Michigan, the Lions blew a 10-0 lead at home, failing to score on four tries from the 1-yard line in a critical series that cost State the game. What's more, the glow of 1982 and '86 glory had begun to wear off. "We haven't been one of the elite teams in the country," Kerry Collins said at the time. "Sure, you want to concentrate just on this game, but in the back of your mind, you know what's riding on it."

History-minded, the Lions had to sense their 16-3 halftime lead that afternoon in Ann Arbor would not hold up. Not in the Big House with 106,832 watching, then the third-largest crowd ever to see a college football game. Michigan's Tyrone Wheatley broke the second play of the third quarter for a 67-yard touchdown run, and after a Penn State punt, Wheatley struck again from 21 yards out to give Michigan a 17-16 lead.

Penn State, which had won each of its first five games by 24 points or more, had to pass the test. Collins responded first, leading a 10-play, 86-yard drive capped by a 9-yard scoring strike to Jon Witman and two-point conversion to Freddie Scott for a 24-17 lead. Michigan clawed back, evening matters at 24 on Tim Biakabutuka's 1-yard run. Then State's offense delivered again. From his own 45, Collins found Engram for a sensational 14-yard grab falling out of bounds. Carter, who finished with 165 yards rushing, busted a 26-yard run. And with 2:53 left in the game, Collins connected with Engram again for a 16-yard touchdown. "I never heard 110,000 people shut up so fast," Marco Rivera said later. When cornerback Brian Miller picked off Michigan quarterback Todd Collins' underthrown pass with 1:32 showing, Penn State could celebrate.

And it did. Thousands of rowdy students back in State College swarmed darkened Beaver Stadium, scaling or sliding beneath fences, some running onto the field to tear up clumps of turf. Others carried an old set of goalposts across campus, while still more gathered outside Paterno's house on McKee Street to await the victorious coach.

The Lions were more composed in the days that followed. They walloped Ohio State 63-14 on Homecoming, then ran the table to finish the regular season 11-0. Of course, as few in and around the program can forget, pollsters moved Nebraska ahead of Penn State at midseason, first in the AP rankings, then in the Coaches' poll. And in the pre-BCS world, No. 2, undefeated Penn State never got a shot at No. 1, undefeated Nebraska, which went on to win the Orange Bowl for the national title one night before Penn State took out Oregon in the Rose Bowl.

"I was never upset," Greeley says now. "I was never mad. It's a popularity contest—a vote. It wasn't decided on the field, and I can't be mad at Nebraska, because they did what we did: won all their games.

"I always felt if I would have been bitter and argued it, it would have demeaned what we did. It would have given credence to guys who never watched us play for real. ... *The New York Times* used to do a computer poll, and we were No. 1 in their poll. People were saying we should declare ourselves *The New York Times* national champions. No. No. We lost. We didn't lose any games, [but] we lost the vote."

Reflecting on State

If there's anything Greeley's bitter about, it's ignorance he says NBC's Bob Costas showed that year when tabbing the network's broadcast of Nebraska-Miami in the Orange Bowl as the national championship game. "These are kids, college kids," says Greeley, who's married with a young daughter and works as a sales rep for insulin manufacturer Novo Nordisk. "We had guys who grew up Penn State fans, whose legacy it was to go play for a national championship. To discount that, to toss that away by making a few flippant remarks, I will never, ever, ever be able to forget that."

Greeley is much more magnanimous about an NFL career cut short by a bruised and lacerated kidney and spleen, a freak injury sustained during a 1998 Steelers-Panthers preseason game. An admitted undersized overachiever, Greeley had toiled on practice squads and sidelines for four years, but he was expected to start that season at center. After sustaining what he describes as "car accident-style trauma" in Pittsburgh, he went seven years before setting foot on another football field, when he returned to State College for the 2005 Blue-White Game, walking onto the Beaver Stadium turf while he and many of his '94 teammates were honored.

Greeley did have NFL tryouts with the Broncos and Giants in '99, and by working out on his own at a YMCA, he says he'd regained his football shape, an accomplishment in and of itself. But one year after the injury, recognizing the stress his NFL dreams were placing on his family, he ditched blocking work for résumé work. After a few years with a small networking firm, he applied his sales skills and health policy and administration degree to land the Novo Nordisk job.

Now, years removed from football, he says it's harder to remember the "warts" of his Penn State days, and easier to recollect the happy times. He especially recounts the potency of that 1994 offense, how each starting offensive lineman had one another's back, and how that unity carried them all to greatness.

"I always feel bad when the defense is left out of the equation," Greeley says. "How many games did they lose us? I want us to be remembered as one of the greatest football teams Penn State has ever had. Football teams. Not offenses, not star power, not scoring ability. Just one of the best *teams*. Cause I think if there's ever a group of guys who epitomized the definition of team, that was the team."

16

JOE NASTASI

NAME: Joseph Eugene Nastasi
BORN: September 27, 1975, in Altoona, Pennsylvania
HOMETOWN: Woodbury, Pennsylvania
CURRENT RESIDENCE: State College, Pennsylvania
OCCUPATION: Co-owner and manager of two State College
    sports bars
POSITION: Wide receiver
HEIGHT: 5 feet, 11 inches
PLAYING WEIGHT: 190 pounds
YEARS LETTERED: 1995 to 1998
NUMBER WORN AT PSU: 21
ACCOMPLISHMENTS: Pennsylvania's Associated Press small
    school high school football player of the year in 1993 was the
    first verbal commitment to Coach Joe Paterno's 1994
    recruiting class; holder for kicker Brett Conway as freshman;
    three-year starter (1996-98) at wide receiver for Penn State;
    co-captain of State's 1998 team that went 9-3; played briefly
    for Cleveland Browns and St. Louis Rams in 1999.
THE GAME: The Snow Bowl, Penn State versus Michigan,
    November 18, 1995

The Young Life of Joe Nastasi

Joe Nastasi didn't need heroes or idols as a kid growing up in Woodbury, Pennsylvania, a tiny dot of land in Bedford County. He had family. And he had sports. He also had values instilled in him by his father, Joe Sr., who taught and coached football at nearby Northern Bedford High, which Joe eventually attended. Sports were a constant. If local kids were around, a game of stickball was usually on. If it was just Joe and younger brother A.J., they'd play one-on-one hoops on the Nastasis' paved porchside basketball court.

"We used to fight every day," Joe says of he and A.J. "We didn't grow up having things or buying things. It was a small area and there wasn't a whole lot going on. Sports were all we had."

Family and sports. At the Nastasis', they were clearly intertwined. Joe Sr., son of a Marine, ran his home with an iron fist, the same way he'd been raised. The impact on son Joe was twofold. Out on the playing fields and courts and inside the classroom, there was no sliding by with excuses. Be it "I'm too tired to finish my homework," or "I'm too winded to run sprints," complaining was out. Joe forgot about looking for crutches to help him through challenges. He simply pushed himself through. Such self-reliance formed the core of a terrific three-sport athlete at Northern Bedford. Joe was a slashing guard on the hoops team; he finished his high school career with 2,961 points, still sixth all time in Pennsylvania prep history. (Brother A.J. tops the list with 3,833 points.) Joe was starting shortstop for the school baseball team. And with his dad on the sideline, he made all-state three times in football, playing five positions as a senior, including quarterback, en route to 1,713 all-purpose yards that season and 5,717 for his career.

Off the field, Joe Sr.'s firm approach helped his son develop into a tough, independent kid who appreciated and cherished his family. "Our family was great," Joe says. "You didn't turn to other people, you turned to each other. You always had dinner together, and you always knew you had that love. ... I didn't always quite understand Dad being so tough, but as I've grown older, I've seen how he made me confident in myself. That went a long way on the football field and a long way in life."

The Setting

Picking a college was easy. Nastasi wanted something close to his hometown so his parents could attend games. Plus he had fond boyhood memories of family trips to Beaver Stadium on fall Saturdays, where he'd memorize the moves of D.J. Dozier and Blair Thomas to mimic them in pickup football games the next day in Woodbury. Penn State was for him, and Nastasi committed in the spring of 1993, while he was a junior in high school. (Such an early commitment was rare at the time in college football.)

Naturally, hailing from a small school and smaller town, there was an adjustment period in the fall of 1994. All those grandiose numbers Nastasi had posted in high school meant nothing now. This was big-time college football, and he was a freshman at a sprawling campus with state-of-the-art football and training facilities. Fortunately any chance of him feeling pressure dissipated when Paterno redshirted the 5-foot, 11-inch speedster. Instead of having to adjust simultaneously to college football and college life, Nastasi, now a full-time wide receiver, spent the year going to class and observing the art of receiving from starting PSU wideouts Bobby Engram and Freddie Scott. He practiced with the squad, running plays with the second- or third-team offense and working with the scout unit. He made friends fast, connecting with teammates like Shawn Lee and Floyd Wedderburn, with whom he remains close today.

The Nittany Lions went undefeated that fall of '94, and Nastasi traveled with the squad to the Rose Bowl, the first time he'd ever been so far from home. In the process, he learned what it meant to play football at Penn State. "We knew how to win," he says. "We had that attitude, which goes a long way. You've gotta understand who you are and get in there and feel that you can't lose."

Such confidence added a precociousness to Nastasi's aura between his freshman and sophomore years. He spent most of the summer of 1995 in State College working out with teammates. Come August, the

Joe Nastasi had other shining moments in his three seasons as a starting wide receiver, but nothing compares to the touchdown he scored on a fake field goal to bury Michigan in the 1995 "Snow Bowl" at Beaver Stadium.

coaching staff trusted him, whether it was as backup to the Engram/Scott/Joe Jurevicius triumvirate or on special teams. Of course, Nastasi could never have foretold how much Paterno & Co. would come to trust him by season's end.

In the fall of '95, he was selected as kicker Brett Conway's holder on field goals and extra points, and held for Conway's game-winner in a 24-23 season-opening victory against Texas Tech. The Nittany Lions started 3-0, then lost to Wisconsin in the Big Ten opener. Six weeks later, a team loaded with Rose Bowl veterans and high hopes for a repeat of 1994's success found itself 6-3 and seeking identity, teetering between recent greatness and newfound conference mediocrity. Big Ten bully Michigan was next on the schedule. Then the snow began to fall.

The Game of My Life
By Joe Nastasi

"THE SNOW BOWL"
PENN STATE VERSUS MICHIGAN
NOVEMBER 18, 1995

At Penn State, we always played hard. Being 6-3 wasn't from lack of effort or lack of coaching. Guys didn't really get down or anything. We knew we were still going to a bowl, we were still going to win out, that kind of thing.

The week of the Michigan game, I remember [then-offensive coordinator] Franny Ganter saying, "Joe, you're gonna be the hero this week." This was on Monday before the game. I was like, "What are you talking about?" He's like, "We'll show you. We have a little something, a little wrinkle we're throwing in." From the beginning, he was like, "This is gonna win us the game." He kept saying it, and we talked about it all that week.

He showed me film and showed me how Michigan overloaded their right side on field goals. He said, "We're gonna use the fake." Cause they had a heavy overload on the right side, and we had a nice little blocking scheme. It wasn't that complicated. We just pulled a guard and kicked the guy out. It was pretty easy.

So that week I remember I was really focused. I was like, "Man, I want to be the hero." But it was one of those things, I didn't know if we were ever going to use it, because a lot of things had to go right.

Then I remember all the snow we got. It was heavy. I remember reading the papers and seeing the stadium. They brought prisoners down to shovel the snow. I knew they'd take care of the field, but I couldn't understand how they were going to get all that snow out of the stands.

When we ran into the stadium for warmups, I looked around. It kind of hits you: Wow, there's a lot of snow up in those stands. I was like, "They're going to be up there throwing snowballs." And they were. I got hit in the back a couple times. Those things were stinging. And it was piled up on the sidelines. Everything was packed in. It was almost like a different stadium, a different place.

Throughout the game, I was waiting for my call. I remember on field goals and extra points, we were giving dummy calls to make sure that when we did call the fake, they didn't have any idea what was going on. We let them know we were definitely kicking. We'd go into the huddle and say "Field goal." But when the fake came, instead of saying "Field goal," I'd say "On me! On me!" Then I'd make the call before the snap. Red meant we were running the fake. Green meant we were kicking it.

There was a time in the fourth quarter when we were going to use it. We were on about their 35-yard line. We were ready to go for the fake, but then Michigan got a 5-yard penalty, offsides or something. Later in the quarter, we got down inside the 10, and on fourth down we called it on the sidelines. We were like, "Okay, here we go, fake field goal." I still had to call it on the field, though. If they weren't lined up in that situation, I would have had to call it off. But they loaded heavy on the one side. They had only three guys on the other. It was easy to see, cause there was such a natural hole there. I counted our guys real quickly as we were lining up. It was perfect. They all went to one side, and all we had to do was account for the guys to our right.

Basically I just took the snap, picked it up and ran. We let two guys come free on the back side and Brett [Conway] just had to get in their way, because it was already going. Everything was right there. It was such a walk-in.

When I scored it was like a flashback. You see all those players before you, all the Penn State history, then all of a sudden here you are scoring on the same field. After that it became like a job-type thing, but that first one was like a fantasy. You can always look back on it and remember that feeling as your first one. The moment's captured. It was like the kid in you coming out and saying man, I scored a touchdown in this stadium.

After the win, I didn't have any idea people would remember the play. Cause anybody could have done it. *Anybody.* It was the simplest play. But I understand it was a big game against Michigan, and it came at a time when we needed it. To this day, people always tell me, "Man, I remember that game in '95..." It was simple, but hey, that's all right. That's how it goes sometimes. I'm glad it was me.

Game Results

Though Michigan was 8-3 and ranked 13th in the nation, No. 19 Penn State was a four-and-a-half-point favorite against the visiting Wolverines for the November 18 showdown at Beaver Stadium. Perhaps the oddsmakers factored in the weather.

By Wednesday night of game week, 19 inches of heavy powder had blanketed State College, a massive storm for so early in the fall. After flirting with the idea of moving the game to Ann Arbor, Michigan, Penn State officials brought in hundreds of volunteers, including students and low-security inmates from area prisons, to clear the field, seats, and walkways. On Saturday, approximately 80,000 fans arrived (96,677 tickets had been sold), many parking miles away in cleared lots and riding shuttle buses to Beaver Stadium.

They were not disappointed. Despite chilly conditions and several game interruptions caused by errantly tossed (or not) snowballs, the two teams combined for 883 yards of total offense. Penn State, its seniors playing their final home game, punched first. The Lions jumped up 10-0 and could have added more in the second quarter, but State fullback Jon Witman fumbled the ball inside Michigan's 10-yard line.

In the second half, State again took a 10-point lead, 20-10, when quarterback Wally Richardson connected with Bobby Engram on a 12-yard touchdown pass. But Michigan, behind the guidance of signal-caller Brian Griese (24 of 46 for 323 yards, one TD), quickly struck back to cut it to 20-17. It was still anyone's game as the clock dwindled.

Clutch play number one was all Stephen Pitts. The senior tailback, who had spelled Ki-Jana Carter and Mike Archie for much of his career, took off for 58 yards to the Michigan 8. For Pitts, it was part of a career-high 164 yards on 17 carries against what was the nation's top rush defense at the time. Clutch play number two was Nastasi's. After Pitts' gallop, State went three and out. With 2:40 left, Penn State lined up for a short field goal, which would have forced Michigan to score a touchdown to win it. But on a snap from the 2-yard line, Nastasi, aided by guard Jeff Hartings' crushing block, sprang through a hole the size of Mt. Nittany and squirted into the end zone. Final score: Penn State 27, Michigan 17.

"I thought we were going to win right up until they converted the fake field goal," Michigan coach Lloyd Carr said afterwards. "It was a great call."

"They didn't want to go out with their tail between their legs," Paterno said of his senior class, which had already lost at home twice that season.

With help from a late Richardson-to-Engram hookup the next week, Penn State beat Michigan State in the regular-season finale to earn a berth in the Outback Bowl on New Year's Day 1996, in which Penn State thrashed Auburn 43-14 to finish 9-3. State's roar was restored, much thanks to the momentum the Lions had been riding since the Snow Bowl.

Reflecting on State

Nastasi graduated Penn State in spring of 1999 with a degree in hotel restaurant management. That fall he gave the NFL a go, signing a free-agent deal with the expansion Cleveland Browns. When he was cut by Cleveland, he caught on briefly with the St. Louis Rams and later had a tryout with the Tampa Bay Buccaneers. Not the biggest receiver in the world, he needed to impress coaches with his speed to have any shot of sticking with a club. But a nagging hamstring slowed his times in the 40, and by 2000, Nastasi had left the league, returned to State College, and become a manager (with a small ownership stake) at the downtown Sports Center Café & Grille, now called Sports Café & Grille.

He and his partner have since opened a second pub on West College Avenue that has a delivery menu and bottle shop. With help from former teammates like NFLers David Macklin and LaVar Arrington, he's stocked both his businesses with plenty of Penn State football merchandise. But the game ball he received that snow-packed day in 1995 is not on display—at least publicly. He keeps it stored in a case in the basement of a house he and his wife recently had built. The ball bears his name, the score and the date. It sits next to a color action photo of the play.

"You take that piece of history with you," says Nastasi, who has a three-year-old son, also named Joe.

In State College, people always ask him about the play. "I just sit there and tell them that was the easiest one I had," Nastasi says. "Cause it's not like I made some move or shook somebody or ran somebody over. It was just one of those things."

One of those things Penn State fans will never be able to wipe from their memory banks.

17

AARON HARRIS

NAME: Aaron Theo Harris
BORN: November 15, 1976, in Coatesville, Pennsylvania
HOMETOWN: Downingtown, Pennsylvania
CURRENT RESIDENCE: West Chester, Pennsylvania
OCCUPATION: Assistant football coach (running backs/travel coordinator), West Chester University
POSITION: Fullback
HEIGHT: 5 feet, 11 inches
PLAYING WEIGHT: 235 pounds
YEARS LETTERED: 1996 to 1999
NUMBER WORN AT PSU: 25
ACCOMPLISHMENTS: Maxwell Club High School Player of the Year in 1994 rushed for 1,800 yards and 32 touchdowns as a senior at Downingtown (Pennsylvania) High; three-year Penn State starter at fullback rushed for 587 yards, nine TDs as a redshirt freshman in 1996; elected team co-captain in 1999; acquired in 2001 by NFL Europe's Berlin Thunder, for which he played one season.
THE GAME: Penn State versus Ohio State, October 11, 1997

The Young Life of Aaron Harris

Aaron Harris should be angry—no, bitter. He should be bitter. Think about it. There was a time Harris owned every football field, a time he could blow through tacklers like leave piles, collecting yards at will. There was a time he was all-everything in high school, then, just months later, he was fulfilling that potential on the grandest of stages. One day, one play, it all changed.

Harris ought to be piping mad, reminiscing about would haves and could haves and should haves 'til he gets a headache. But he isn't saying or doing any of that. No spite. No pity pleas. And those who know him best, his friends and family, would not expect different from him. Harris always was the rare sports star who refused to pin his life's dreams on making the bucks and obtaining the bling that goes hand in hand with the bright lights of the NFL. For him, there's always been more to life.

It's a perspective that came to him first from his folks, Paula and William. Born in Coatesville, Pennsylvania, and raised in nearby Downingtown since sixth grade, Aaron, older brother Andre, and younger brother Arlen grew up in a household with strict rules. No TV. No video games. You took care of your chores.

"They just didn't want us ruled by a lot of the images," says Harris, who still shares a close bond with his siblings and parents. "From chores and morals to how you act in public and on the field, they definitely wanted Godly young men."

Aaron grew rapidly after taking up organized football at age eight. He played a year in Coatesville before joining the Downingtown Young Whippets, mimicking moves he internalized watching Walter Payton on TV. In eighth grade he surpassed the midget league's 140-pound weight limit: "Come home from school, four peanut butter and jelly sandwiches, glass of milk, go to sleep," he says, explaining his growth spurt.

In ninth grade Harris was physically and athletically ahead of his peers, and he proved it by starting and holding his own as a freshman running back on Downingtown High's varsity squad. During the ensuing three years he lifted his school to state powerhouse status,

Aaron Harris certainly lived through highs and lows in his Nittany Lion career: His 51-yard cutback rumble ignited Penn State's 1997 comeback victory against Ohio State; the torn ACL he sustained a week later slowed a career heavy on NFL potential.

helping it earn a berth in the 1994 Class Four-A state title game against McKeesport, whose best player, Brandon Short, later became Harris' teammate at Penn State.

Harris' unassuming, relaxed attitude was already evident. When reporters asked about squaring off against Short in the championship, "I said, 'Who?'" Harris says. "His team gave him flak about that, but I actually didn't know. It was just about our team." (McKeesport won the game, and Short was sure to tease Harris about it when they became Penn State freshmen in 1995.)

For Harris, college was about education. Case in point? A closet computer geek who learned his first skills on the family's Commodore, he selected colleges based on their computer science programs. Here was a kid who rushed for nearly 2,000 yards his senior year of high school, with offers from Michigan, Tennessee, Notre Dame, and others, checking out labs and job placement records. After he and his parents spent their own money on an exploratory college road trip in the summer of 1994, Harris chose Penn State. He was there to learn, but the football limelight beckoned.

The Setting

Harris was 5 feet, 11 inches and 210 pounds when he arrived for school in 1995. Perfect for a tailback. Not perfect for a Big Ten fullback. Initially Penn State offensive coordinator Fran Ganter had Harris practice at tailback alongside veterans Mike Archie, Stephen Pitts, and fellow frosh Chafie Fields. But that September, Harris learned he'd be redshirted and switched to fullback. "I ended up on the scout team," he says. "Took all kinds of bumps and bruises, cause we had some really good linebackers: Aaron Collins, Jim Nelson, Brandon Short. They were hittin' the mess out of me."

Harris, showing resiliency he'd call on in the future, assumed the right attitude. He just wanted to play, and if that meant embracing the fullback job, he'd bulk up (he jumped to 235 pounds in '96), learn the formations, and improve as a blocker. It was a good thing, too, because Coach Joe Paterno promised him he wouldn't carry the ball if he didn't learn how to block. When his redshirt freshman season got rolling the next fall, Harris found himself clearing lanes for Curtis Enis, a converted linebacker who fluctuated between 230 and 260 pounds while at State—always bigger than Harris. It was a dominating twosome, both in size and flexibility.

"We did a lot more single-back stuff, cause they knew I could block. But I was also a bit of a threat to just bust one and go," says Harris, foreshadowing his greatest play in blue and white. "That kept everybody honest, and we could use Curt wherever we wanted."

Enis and Harris logged a combined 1,797 yards and 22 touchdowns on the ground in 1996. Their power game exhausted opposing front sevens, and it was on the strength of such ground muscle that *Sports Illustrated* picked Penn State preseason No. 1 the summer before the 1997 season. The fabled *SI* cover jinx would strike that fall, but not before Ohio State arrived in early October to offer the 4-0 Nittany Lions their first real test of the schedule.

The Game of My Life
By Aaron Harris

PENN STATE VERSUS OHIO STATE
OCTOBER 11, 1997

Believe it or not, I never cared about being No. 1. It was like high school when they asked about Brandon. I wasn't ignorant to it, but it was like, preseason No. 1, okay, that does nothing for us. We gotta go out and prove it each week. I'd rather put my time into studying plays or lifting.

That year we knew the first four games (Pitt, Temple, Louisville, and Illinois) were kind of warmup games. So we went out and handled business, and felt real good about ourselves. We were getting into a groove.

In practice for Ohio State, we were going for it. We knew they were the doorkeepers to our season. The year before against Ohio State, we'd gotten murdered. We went out there and had no clue. They beat us up in every phase of the game. So in '97, we thought, we're the best team. We have to beat 'em. For last year, for the season, for everything. It was personal.

We always laugh, cause (Buckeyes linebacker Andy) Katzenmoyer and the whole linebacker crew came out that day with black visors. After I scored the first touchdown, the black visors were gone. There were probably four equipment managers over there yanking at their helmets. I guess they came out and thought they could be pretty with visors. We came out and said, "Let's just play some football."

Speaking of Katzenmoyer, everything we did, we aimed at him. Everybody had tried to go around him, but he was such a good player at that position, he could probably stay with anybody. So we went straight at him. I was hitting him, [tight end] Brad Scioli was hitting him, Curt, [fullback] Anthony Cleary. Cut him, hit him in the mouth, turn his shoulders. Do whatever you gotta do.

When we went up 10-0, because of the way we had driven down, [we knew it was going] to be a good day. By the third quarter, that whole feeling changed. Our sideline was quiet. Everybody in the stands was quiet. We were flustered to the point where we looked lost, like we're letting this slip away.

It was called "36 slant." That was the play they loved giving to me. It was Curt leading as a blocker. This time he ended up being part of a double team, cause our guard also got to Katzenmoyer. All day that play had been bouncing outside, so I said I'll just take it up the middle. I ended up getting Ping-Ponged around a little. There were two defensive backs about to wipe me up, but when they hit me, it spun me and put me right past them. After that, it was all instincts. Next thing I know there's [quarterback] Mike McQueary in front of me leading me down the field. Nobody else.

I didn't really hear the crowd 'til I scored, but that place erupted. We were still down, but it put some life in people. Next thing you know, our defense gets a turnover, we go down and score again. Ohio State still had a chance to do some things against us, but our defense manned up and was up to the task.

It was close in the end, but we pulled it out. I think it gives character to a team when you go through the good ones like that and come out victorious.

Game Results

On an unusually warm October afternoon in Central Pennsylvania, a then Beaver Stadium-record crowd of 97,282 fans witnessed perhaps the game of the year in college football. Penn State, behind a bullish offensive line and the Enis-Harris combination, dominated the ground to the tune of 316 yards rushing. Going the other way, Buckeye Joe Germaine threw for 378 yards and two touchdowns to keep Penn State's secondary backpedaling all day. Put it together and you had a seesaw affair.

A Harris touchdown and Travis Forney field goal made it 10-0 midway through the first. Ohio State answered with a Dan Stultz field goal and a Germaine-to-Dee Miller TD pass of 35 yards. And on it went. The play of the game, Harris' rumble, occurred late in the third after Ohio State had erased a 17-13 halftime deficit with touchdowns by wideout David Boston and running back Pepe Pearson.

It was an electrifying 51-yard adventure. Harris bounced in and out of traffic, gaining speed as he trucked for the right pylon in the south end zone. His score made it 27-24 Buckeyes, and Penn State took the lead for good, 31-27, at 10:31 in the fourth on Enis' 26-yard touchdown (he finished with 211 yards rushing). From there a Penn State defensive effort killed off three late Buckeye drives.

As fans howled in the night, Enis welled with tears of relief while answering questions in the media room. That was the high. The low came seven days later against Minnesota. In that game, Harris caught a pass on a busted screen play, broke into the open field and tried to cut, the grass slipping then grasping hold of his cleat, causing the fullback to hyperextend his right knee. Harris took a vicious blow from Minnesota's Tyrone Carter on the play, but he credits that shot for lifting him off his leg and preventing further damage to the knee. As it was, he'd already torn his ACL.

"I'd never had pain like that; I didn't even try to get up," Harris says. "I had to crutch all the way off. They laid me down in the locker room. Then my family came in. My dad's not a talkative person. He's real quiet. But he leaned over and said, 'We'll get through this.' That's when the floodgates opened. I knew the season was chalked up."

State came back to nip the Gophers 16-15, but the Lions never truly recovered, losing at home to Michigan two games later—Harris, drugged from surgery that same day, told his mom he wanted to play against the Wolverines—to Michigan State in the season finale and and to Florida in the Citrus Bowl. From 7-0 to 9-3, just like that.

Harris' recovery was equally painful. Rather than submit to missing 1998 and seeking an additional redshirt season, he pushed for a speedy return, rolling to classes in a wheelchair and later hobbling on crutches (Enis used to escort him to classes), all the while punishing his body to bounce back.

He played '98 with a bulky knee brace, rushing for 112 yards as a slower, less-sure form of his old self. He was better brace-less in '99. Harris even says he felt all the way back early that senior year, but by then he was suffering from undiagnosed rheumatoid arthritis. "By the Alamo Bowl, I couldn't walk," says Harris, who had pulled himself out of the 1999 regular-season finale against Michigan State a month earlier. "Everybody was trying to dress me. It was bad.

"I told them I didn't even want to warm up. Cause once everybody ran out on the field, you know how fast we come out, and I was struggling to keep up. I told one of the scout team players, 'Whatever you do, don't leave me. Don't make me look like that guy limping in the back who's dead weight to the team.'"

Reflecting on State

Harris, so full of promise early in his career, never played a down in the Alamo Bowl, his final game as a college fullback. He took himself out after warmups. "Some of the coaches thought I was quitting on the team," he says of his final two college games, "but nobody would diagnose me." He went undrafted, and in 2000 he took his integrative arts degree and moved to New York City, finding work as a consultant and graphic designer for *SmartMoney.com*, *WinMill*, and *Women.com*. But even his desk jobs grew laborious. He was constantly sleepy. It pained him to walk. Once, while visiting younger brother Arlen at the University of Virginia, he failed trying to bench press 135 pounds.

Life for Harris improved drastically in 2001 when an arthritis specialist in West Chester prescribed a new drug called Remicade. Within two weeks Harris was lifting and running. He felt so good that he played a season of NFL Europe in Berlin, doing well enough to earn tryouts with the NFL's Eagles, Jets, and Broncos. (He pulled a hamstring in one of the tryouts, slowing his times and ruining his shot at making any of the teams.)

Through everything, Harris never lingered on the past. Still doesn't. When football wasn't to be, he began coaching, then teaching. Downingtown. Valley Forge. Coatesville, where he met his eventual wife, Courtney. They married in July 2005. Now at West Chester, he's hands-on, breaking down film, running and stretching with players, recruiting, teaching Paterno's suit-and-tie principles of acting responsible on and off the field.

"I keep trying to tell these kids," he says, "whatever you do, don't let football use you. Use football. Cause football's always going to be a platform for them."

It has been for Harris. His run against Ohio State will never be forgotten, nor will talk of how good he could have been if not for that ACL tear one afternoon in Beaver Stadium. Harris has heard all the talk, but he won't look back, "cause if you're looking back," he says, "you can't go forward."

"Some family members are like, 'Oh, you can still make it,'" he continues. "I'm like, 'Even if I could, how long is it going to last? One game? One year?' There's a lot of other things you can enjoy and keep the sport in your life."

One of those things is life itself.

18

LaVAR ARRINGTON

NAME: LaVar RaShad Arrington
BORN: June 20, 1978, in Pittsburgh, Pennsylvania
HOMETOWN: Pittsburgh, Pennsylvania
CURRENT RESIDENCE: Annapolis, Maryland
OCCUPATION: NFL linebacker, New York Giants
POSITION: Outside linebacker
HEIGHT: 6 feet, 3 inches
PLAYING WEIGHT: 240 pounds
YEARS LETTERED: 1997 to 1999
NUMBER WORN AT PSU: 11
ACCOMPLISHMENTS: In 1998, he became the first sophomore
to win Big Ten Defensive Player of the Year honors, finishing
second on the team in tackles (67, including 17 for a loss),
breaking up 11 passes and intercepting two more; 12th two-
time first-team All-American in school history won the Butkus
Award (top linebacker) and Chuck Bednarik Award (nation's
top defensive player) in 1999; won Alamo Bowl Defensive
MVP his final collegiate game; had 72 tackles (20 for a loss),
nine sacks, one interception and two blocked kicks in '99;
Selected second overall by the Washington Redskins in 2000
NFL draft; he's made three Pro Bowls.
THE GAME: The Alamo Bowl, Penn State versus Texas A&M,
December 28, 1999

The Young Life of LaVar Arrington

LaVar Arrington is shy. Always was. Oh sure, the former Penn State linebacker will knock you dizzy on the field. And he's known to speak freely to the media, whether he's quoting Joe Paterno or Joe Gibbs. What makes him different, what's helped shape his meteoric football career, is a realization that being shy can hurt. "Being personable has a lot to do with how people perceive you," says Arrington, who was named after *Roots* actor LeVar Burton. "If you're too shy, people don't have an opportunity to get to know the type of person you are."

So despite his reserved inner self, the Pittsburgh, Pennsylvania, native has been quick to speak up with opportunities at hand. When he was eight years old and playing his first football for the Westview Braves, Arrington chafed at having to toil on the offensive and defensive lines. After all, his father, Michael, who lost his left leg and right foot when he was run over by a tank in Vietnam, used to spend hours showing LaVar footage of the greats: Walter Payton, Gale Sayers, Eric Dickerson. LaVar wanted to carry the ball. And eventually, he got his way.

Arrington didn't back down in grade school either. He wasn't looking for trouble, but when kids singled him out for being bigger than others his age, and names, sometimes racially tinged, were fired in his direction, Arrington swung back. "It would get to a point where [I would think], 'Let me go ahead and knock you out so you don't mess with me,'" he says. "I would try to make an example of somebody so I didn't have to do it anymore."

Fights flared up so frequently at school that Michael and LaVar's mother, Carolyn, a special education teacher, pulled LaVar from his predominantly all-white school and sent him to a different school in Pittsburgh. There he says he found himself fighting for his lunch money rather than his reputation.

Arrington, the second of three sons, looked up to older brother Michael, a skilled basketball player. LaVar had hops too, and that seemed the direction he was headed when he got to high school.

LaVar Arrington, the 1999 Butkus Award winner, was a quarterback's nightmare in his three seasons at Penn State. In 1999 the then junior linebacker collected nine sacks to finish with 19 for his career; he also won defensive MVP honors in that season's Alamo Bowl.

Granted, he loved the Steelers—former Steelers defensive lineman Dwight White was one of his neighbors and mentors growing up— and he revered local football legends who'd played at schools like Westinghouse, Penn Hills, and Perry. (Years later LaVar would name his son, Keeno, after a star prep quarterback that LaVar had idolized as a kid.)

While at North Hills High, Arrington began receiving buckets of letters with basketball offers. The problem was he didn't like being typecast as a physical player, like the "banger" sixth man role he filled for his Pittsburgh Jots traveling team. "I didn't want to just be average," says Arrington, who, as a prep player, balled against future NBAers Stephon Marbury, Danny Fortson, and Lamar Odom. "Being from a football city, I felt like I could achieve more and earn more respect playing football."

Football offers also streamed in for the 6-foot, 3-inch, 220-pound running back/linebacker who rushed for 4,357 yards and 72 touchdowns at North Hills. He received his first football interest letters, from Miami and Notre Dame, as an eighth-grader. Arrington also loved Florida State and the stars the Seminoles had produced, but in the end, he wanted to stay close to his tight-knit family. It was either Pitt or Penn State.

"One day just on a humbug, my mom and dad said, 'Let's go up and look at Penn State,'" Arrington says. "[The Penn State coaches] find out I'm in town visiting. Joe Paterno, who was in Washington D.C. visiting President Clinton, jumps on a charter plane and flies home to Penn State to meet with me. Needless to say, I committed that weekend. It's like, you were with the president and you jumped on a plane to see me? Man, done deal. I'm coming."

That was the high point in the relationship between Arrington and Paterno.

The Setting

Some freshmen are quiet, patient, eager to play but satisfied to wait. That's key at Penn State, where upperclassmen and loyalty have long been staples of Paternoism. But Arrington was different.

He says he was told before the 1997 season that he'd be given an opportunity to play right away, and when it didn't happen, he took it hard. Who cares that established upperclassmen like Aaron Collins and Jim Nelson were starters? Certainly not Arrington. He was special. He didn't need a year of adjustment.

"I felt like they had lied to me," he says, referring to the coaching staff. "There's a whole bunch of other universities I could have gone to and started as a freshman."

Arrington's first response was to prove everyone wrong, show so much burst and power that they'd have to play him. Special teams or nickel backer, when he hit the field, opponents hit the turf. "It's egos, man," he says. "A lot of people say the greats have egos. They can't let people be better than them. I think that's what pushes you. So I kept pushing. Every time I got an opportunity, I'd try to knock somebody's head off."

His talent was evident, but it didn't spell additional reps for Arrington. As his freshman year drew to a close, the star linebacker, perhaps for the first time in his life, began to doubt himself. He used to sit and cry in his dorm room. He'd cry about the future; about wasting an opportunity at an NFL career. He was trying to buck a legendary septuagenarian's 40-year-old system, and he was losing.

In the spring of 1998, he pondered transferring. Seriously. He had a spectacular spring practice and could have been an incumbent starter at nearly any other school. Still, he remained stuck behind Aaron Gatten on the depth chart. Paterno was dead serious. And JoePa could argue that his plan worked, too, seeing as how Arrington wasn't the opening game starter in 1998, yet wound up winning Big Ten Defensive Player of the Year that season for 9-3 Penn State.

Of course, by then it was too late for LaVar and Joe. Arrington was going to play like a madman in 1999, but by then he'd be playing for himself. The NFL dream was already dancing about his brain. Another All-American season like the one he had in '98 would send him on his way. With that attitude, it made sense that a "shy" Arrington would open up to *Sports Illustrated* in the summer of '99—he graced the cover of that issue—a move he now semi-regrets.

"They do things a certain way around here," he told the magazine, which ranked Penn State No. 1 that preseason. "I don't think that's going to win you many national titles, not in 1999 or 2000. Athletes have evolved. To win a national title, you put your best athletes out there and you let them play with emotion and intensity. You don't change them."

Said Paterno of Arrington in the same piece: "He's not even our best player. He might not even be our best linebacker. ... He has great potential, but that's all. People want me to say he's the best linebacker I've ever coached. Put him in the same class as Shane Conlan and Jack Ham? You've got to be kidding. Someday he might be all those things."

The feud lived throughout the '99 season, overshadowed temporarily by Penn State's 9-0 start and shocking 0-3 finish, a collapse ignited by a freakish play at Beaver Stadium on which a batted pass and catch set up Minnesota's game-winning field goal in the Gophers' improbable 24-23 upset of the Nittany Lions.

Arrington pins that loss on fate. Eight weeks later in the Alamo Bowl, he and his mates would leave nothing to chance. Not in his final collegiate game.

The Game of My Life
By LaVar Arrington

THE ALAMO BOWL
PENN STATE VERSUS TEXAS A&M
DECEMBER 28, 1999

In 1999, from top to bottom, offensively and defensively, there wasn't a more talented bunch of guys. For three or four years, we had No. 1, No. 2 recruiting classes. You figure you should be spanking cats. I'm coming in with Curtis Enis and Aaron Harris in the backfield. Brandon Short, Courtney Brown, and David Macklin were already there. There's no way you can tell me we should be losing to anybody. But for whatever reason, it didn't materialize. I mean I could say it, but it's not worth it. I think it was pretty clear why we didn't reach our full potential.

Personally, I dealt with a lot that year. The Minnesota loss? My dad had to come get me out of the locker room after the game. Then I got hurt against Michigan. A-Train [Wolverines running back Anthony Thomas] knocked my shoulder out of my socket. And of course, all along Joe [Paterno] went hard trying to convince people not to talk to me about being the best linebacker in America. I don't know what Joe had against me, but he made sure to talk about Courtney [Brown]. I don't have a problem with you campaigning for another player, but don't make it between LaVar and Courtney. Everyone wanted to call me a brash individual because I spoke my mind, but all of a sudden you come up with a plan to make Courtney the quiet storm, playing off that he's quiet and I'm not. That's a direct attack on me.

So I came into the Alamo Bowl trying to prove to every man, woman, and child who the best defensive player in America was. That was my whole frame of thought. And I already knew that was my last game. I thought about coming back, but for like two seconds. Why would I return? If [defensive coordinator] Jerry Sandusky would have come back, then my decision would have been different. I owe everything to Jerry Sandusky. That was my guy. I enjoyed college and I wanted to see what I could do in one more year, but Jerry was the deciding factor. When he was retiring, I decided I wasn't coming back.

That was motivation, too, in the Alamo Bowl. Win it for Jerry, man. Cause if anybody deserved something great to happen to him, it's Jerry Sandusky. So our defense came out with the intent of sending Jerry out that way. And we were clicking on all cylinders. We took their heart, man. We were killing them. And I don't want to cause a controversy from years past, but Rashard Casey was the starting quarterback that day—[it] made a huge difference in our offensive production.

That team went from getting ready to play for a national title— we were on a crash course with Florida State—to not even playing on New Year's Day. So it meant a lot to go out there and thrash those boys like we did. It kind of validated us.

When they took me out toward the end of the game, my whole career at Penn State, my whole life, started to flash by me. It was like, this is it. Then Joe came up to me on the sideline and said, "Are you leaving?" I said, "Yeah, I'm out of here." He was like, "You're ready. You'll be all right." Everything that we had gone through, all the hard times and ups and downs, at the end of the day we still respected one another a great deal. That's what meant the most to me that day. He didn't have to tell the media. I didn't care if he told the world. As long as he acknowledged it to me.

Game Results

Texas A&M ran into the wrong Penn State team on December 28, 1999, in the Alamo Bowl in San Antonio. Fuming from a 9-0 start to 9-3 plummet, Penn State coaches challenged players to prove their abilities as athletes. This was about identity. Said Arrington: "I think people forgot what kind of team we were."

Before an Alamo Bowl-record 65,380 fans in the final game of Jerry Sandusky's 23-year run as Nittany Lions defensive coordinator, his defense was the stuff of dreams. On A&M's first pass play of the game, Arrington, the '99 Butkus Award winner, popped Aggies quarterback Randy McCown as he threw, the ball fluttering into the arms of David Macklin. State couldn't capitalize when Travis Forney missed a field goal, but on the next A&M series, McCown was picked again, this time by safety Derek Fox, who weaved 34 yards for the first points of the game.

In the second quarter, Rashard Casey, who had outplayed regular starter Kevin Thompson in practice, hooked up with Eddie Drummond for a 45-yard pass play and a 14-0 PSU lead. That was more than enough for an already loose and aggressive State D. Arrington was the catalyst, collecting 14 tackles and a sack that night and harassing McCown nearly every time he dropped back.

In the third, down 14-0, the Aggies still had life. They were on the State 14-yard line, but on a critical third-down play, Arrington tipped McCown's pass into the arms of linebacker Ron Graham. And before being lifted in the fourth, Arrington flattened McCown once more to halt an Aggies drive. Penn State sealed the game when Casey took it in from 4 yards out on a naked bootleg. A Forney field goal made the final 24-0 State.

The victory marked the first time the Nittany Lions had pitched a bowl game shutout since a 7-0 victory against Alabama in the 1959 Liberty Bowl. The numbers? State held the Aggies to 202 total yards of offense, intercepted four passes, and recovered a fumble. Oh yeah, and the Lions carried one deserving coach off the field after 32 years of service on State's staff. "This whole season has been such an emotional experience," said Sandusky, game ball in hand. "I didn't plan on any grand exit, but I got one.

"The warmth of the football players, the former football players, the Penn State fans—it has all been so special."

Reflecting on State

Arrington, whom Michigan coach Lloyd Carr once compared to Hall of Famer Lawrence Taylor, has not disappointed in his pro career, though there is much more he wants to do before he leaves the game. Drafted second overall in 1999 behind teammate Courtney Brown, he made three Pro Bowls with the Redskins, brandishing the athleticism and big-play ability that won him accolades and attention at Penn State. But it's been frustrating, too. The Skins changed defensive coordinators each of his first five seasons in the pros, leaving him confused and uncertain as to the team's direction and his role on the field. When knee surgery and rehab sidelined him for most of the 2004 season (he had a second scope in 2005), he heard trade rumors fueled by Washington's stout defensive play in his absence. In 2005 he spent more minutes than he'd care to count riding the bench, then decided in early 2006 to sever ties with Washington to pursue a new team. (He eventually signed a multiyear deal with the New York Giants.)

"My pro career makes me cherish, respect, and love every moment of a Joe Paterno and Jerry Sandusky and Penn State experience," says Arrington, who got married in 2005 and says he intends to complete his degree someday. "I didn't agree with everything Joe did, but the man was a hell of a person in terms of teaching us how to be men. Honestly, I don't know that I would have been able to handle the situations I'm in now if I hadn't had Joe doing to me the things that he did."

Perhaps not surprising, though, Arrington has hardly spoken to Paterno since leaving State College. He says he's tried to reach out, even called, left his numbers for Joe during the leaner times of the past five years. But nothing. To Arrington's credit, it hasn't soured the standout linebacker on Penn State. He's still tight with Sandusky and Penn Staters in the pros. Catch him in a TV interview, and you might see him wearing a PSU hat or shirt or flashing that Nittany Lion inked into his arm.

"Regardless how it turned out or the way I feel or anybody else feels, I did it within the rules, but I did it my way," Arrington says. "I don't have any reason to feel bad about where I went to school. I have a Penn State tattoo that I'll never get rid of. I'll love Penn State forever."

He isn't shy about that.

19

ZACK MILLS

NAME: Zachary Eric Mills
BORN: May 1, 1982, in Rockville, Maryland
HOMETOWN: Ijamsville, Maryland
CURRENT RESIDENCE: Philadelphia, Pennsylvania
OCCUPATION: Graduate assistant coach at Temple University
POSITION: Quarterback
HEIGHT: 6 feet, 3 inches
PLAYING WEIGHT: 214 pounds
YEARS LETTERED: 2001 to 2004
NUMBER WORN AT PSU: 7
ACCOMPLISHMENTS: Finished prep career with 59
    touchdowns, 5,638 passing yards at Urbana High; at Penn
    State, threw for 41 career touchdowns, tied for most in
    school history; owns 18 different Penn State offensive records,
    including most career pass attempts (1,082), completions
    (606), passing yards (7,212), and total yards (7,796); also
    owns the top Penn State freshman (1,669) and sophomore
    (2,417) single-season passing totals; 399-yard day versus Iowa
    in 2002 is a single-game school passing record.
THE GAME: Penn State versus Ohio State, October 27, 2001

The Young Life of Zack Mills

The name Zack Mills conjures mixed emotions among Nittany Lions faithful. Some fans loved him. Others loved to boo him. After all, in the five years Mills spent in University Park, he witnessed, at times even embodied, the sweet elevations and ugly depths of a traditional college football power in flux.

In Mills' estimation, simply getting to Happy Valley, let alone playing such a pivotal role in the team's fortunes for four seasons, was improbable enough a feat. Especially when you consider that he hated football when he began playing, and that as late as his junior year at Maryland's Urbana High, he was a blip on recruiting radars nationwide.

"The coaches had us doing crazy tackling drills, where everyone would be in a circle and they'd pick two guys to run outside the circle and hit each other," says Mills of his first football experience, as a fifth-grader. "I remember coming home all bruised up and not wanting to go back."

Initially a linebacker and tailback, Mills moved to quarterback in sixth grade. During the next five years he developed at the position, but certainly not to the point of coveted prospect status. It wasn't until fall of 1998 that Mills, the son of a construction manager, first realized football could carry him to a free education at a top-level program. He was an Associated Press first-team small-school all-state pick that year, topping 2,000 yards passing to carry Urbana to the Maryland Class 2A state title. That same fall, without Mills' knowledge, Urbana coach Dave Carruthers sent tapes of the southpaw to Penn State defensive line coach Larry Johnson. The PSU assistant, who'd spent the first 17 years of his career in Maryland's high school ranks and had coached against Carruthers, was impressed. So was Penn State coach Joe Paterno. "Supposedly," Mills says, "Joe looked at a couple minutes' worth and said, 'We have to offer this kid.'"

Thus, in the winter of his junior year of high school, Mills was handed the telephone by Carruthers. Johnson, holding on the other line, passed his phone to Paterno. "He started talking about full grant in aid, books, room and board," Mills recalls. "I was in shock. He's

Zack Mills remains atop the school record book for passing yards (7,212), but in 2001, the then freshman quarterback used his legs to bring the Nittany Lions back against Ohio State and help Joe Paterno gain career win No. 324.

like, 'Take some time and think about it. It's early.' I got off the phone, and I still wasn't sure if he had offered me or not. I was just so in awe. So when [Carruthers] was like, 'Well?' I said, 'I think they offered me some money, but I don't know for sure.' He called Larry back just to verify."

No joke. Penn State wanted Mills, but Paterno was pursuing quarterbacks Jeff Smoker and Zac Wasserman, too. The coach wanted two of the three, so when Wasserman verballed in March 1999, Mills quickly followed suit. His first chance to shine at State was less than 24 months away.

The Setting

Mills joined a program that had not lost more than three games in a season for seven straight years. Losing records? Try one since 1938. But things changed in 2000, as the Lions stumbled to a 1-4 start while Mills redshirted and watched Rashard Casey battle lingering legal troubles (an aggravated assault charge the previous spring, of which Casey was later cleared) and disgruntled fans. "It was like, wow, what's going on?" says Mills of his freshman year, when Penn State finished 5-7. "I didn't regret that I came, but being new to the program, I was confused why all of a sudden we weren't playing well."

The silver lining? For Mills, it was a learning experience. He noted that Casey never complained about his off-field troubles, and how the senior dealt with media queries into whether he should be playing amid the legal situation. Mills also began devouring State's offense with help from new friend Matt Senneca, Casey's backup.

Following 2001 spring ball, fellow freshman Wasserman left school to move closer to his mother, whom he learned had been diagnosed with breast cancer. Mills was thrust into Senneca's backup role. "You don't want to see someone leave for those reasons," says Mills of Wasserman, "but it opened a door for me."

It was a quick rise for the rookie. In August of '01, when Senneca, penciled in as the starter, missed practice with a sore arm, Mills found himself taking snaps with the first team. Recognizing Mills' inexperience, Paterno challenged him, pressured him, argued with him over the smallest of details even when Mills was in the right. If Mills would someday be throwing footballs on Saturdays before 100,000 fans, he'd first prove his mettle before Paterno's thick lenses.

Paterno's focus on his backup quarterback proved worthwhile. On September 1, 2001, with Penn State down 10-0 in the first quarter to the stacked Miami Hurricanes at sold-out and newly expanded Beaver Stadium, Senneca ran to the sideline, complaining he couldn't feel his arm. "They're like, 'Mills, Mills, go in!'" he recalls of his first college game. "I'd put my helmet behind one of the benches, but when I went running to find it, I couldn't. We had to burn a timeout." Mills eventually joined the huddle and called a pass play, on which he got crushed, he says.

That summed up the evening: Penn State dropped its opener 33-7 to the Hurricanes of Ken Dorsey, Clinton Portis, & Co. For Mills, however, it was the start of something. Because while Senneca sat out the remainder of the game, Mills began growing comfortable in the pocket, finishing with 240 yards passing and a touchdown toss to Bryant Johnson.

Ten days later, on 9/11, the world changed. Business, travel, football—it all ceased. Penn State, slated for a Thursday night game at Virginia, rescheduled it for December and didn't play again until September 22, an 18-6 home loss to Wisconsin, a game Senneca started. Mills says he would have been content to watch from the sideline the rest of that season, a redshirt freshman awaiting an upperclassman's job. But the script kept changing, and Penn State's slide continued—0-3, then 0-4. Senneca was a good friend to Mills, but it was becoming increasingly evident that he was not the answer to State's ills. On October 20, after a bye week, Senneca compiled his best game as a Nittany Lion in a shootout with Northwestern. But with less than two minutes remaining in the road game and State driving deep in Wildcat territory, Senneca took a big-league wallop and was knocked out of the game.

Summoned again, Mills jogged into the huddle and famously asked the offense, "What's up, fellas? You ready to take this in?" Then, on a play Paterno himself called, Mills hit running back Eric McCoo from 4 yards out to salvage a dramatic 38-35 victory, State's first of 2001 and Paterno's career 323rd, tying him with Bear Bryant in Division I-A history. "You would have thought we were 5-0," Mills says. "Guys were so relieved to finally get a win. That game was huge."

The next week's home contest against Ohio State, with Paterno poised to break Bryant's mark, was even bigger for Mills.

The Game of My Life
By Zack Mills

PENN STATE VERSUS OHIO STATE, OCTOBER 27, 2001

Matt was back. He missed a couple days of practice [after Northwestern], but he was back and they decided he was going to start. They told me I was going to get to play. They told me to be ready, and I'm thinking, yeah, okay.

We get to the game and Matt plays one series. Joe's like, "Zack, go in." I'm like, "Are you serious?" A week earlier he'd told me to get ready like 12 times. This time, very first series, I'm going in. It helped that I'd had Monday and Tuesday with the first team. So mentally I was aware of different things, like their blitz and cover schemes.

Early on we had gone down, gotten in the red zone, stalled out, and couldn't punch it in. [We had only scored] three field goals. Robbie Gould was a true freshman, and he was kicking really well. Later, even when we were down, I didn't feel panicked because we were able to move the football. When you're struggling offensively, going three and out and have about 100 yards of total offense at halftime— it's those games when you start to worry a little in the back of your mind. You might start to press. That wasn't the case. I remember we had a lot of success between the 20 and 20, we just couldn't punch it in. I knew if we kept doing what we were doing, we'd get down there again, and we'd eventually punch it in.

One thing people forget is I threw three picks. One in the second quarter that was a pretty bad pass, a Hail Mary at the end of the half, then the one that got us. It was play-action bootleg. I came around and Eddie Drummond was *wide* open. If you look at it on tape, he would have had about a 30-, 40-yard gain. But it went right off his hands, flying in the air. That's when you wish a gust of wind would just knock the ball down. Cause you see it happening. [Buckeyes safety Derek] Ross got it and ran right to the end zone.

It was 27-9. Joe was all over Eddie. He didn't play the rest of the day. People were coming up to me like, "It's all right. You'll get 'em back." I'm fine at this point, because there's nothing I can do. I can't catch the ball for him. I can just throw it. So I was like, "All right, let's get the ball back and see what we can do."

The next possession, we were in the shotgun and it was an option right with (running back) Larry [Johnson]. I think the call was "Lucky Gun 2 Speed." And the defender went with Larry, so I tucked it up. Everyone remembers me jumping over (offensive lineman Chris) McKelvy. Then someone blocked Ross into me, and I bounced off Ross right after I came off that hop. That kind of propelled me forward, and the next thing I know, I was running as fast as I could. At one point right before I got (to the end zone), I almost tripped. My stride got a little messed up because I tried to look up at the screen to see if anyone was behind me.

When I scored, that fired everyone up. If we had gone three and out on that drive, that might have been the ballgame. It would have taken the wind out of the defense.

We scored again off a turnover. Someone fumbled and Shawn Mayer recovered. We ran a bootleg for a 20-yard pass to Bryant Johnson. A few plays later I hit Tony Johnson in the corner of the end zone for a touchdown.

Our next drive started in the third quarter and ended in the fourth. We had a couple third-down conversions plus the play when the ball went over my head and I ran back there, picked it up, and when I didn't see anyone, I tried to bootleg around. Everyone was coming at me on an angle, so I ran around them and R.J. Luke was just standing there, wide open. A few plays later we ran the same play to McCoo that we scored on against Northwestern. Same way, too. It was on the lefthand side, and we got him matched up on a linebacker. He went out, then up, and caught the ball and scored, and it got us ahead.

After we had the blocked field goal and hung on, the team was fired up and happy as can be that Joe broke the record. I remember I was just standing there, trying to take it all in. Everyone was mobbing Joe. But I remember being outside of it. I knew it was a day that would be remembered for a long time by a lot of people. I played my part in it, and I'm proud of myself for the way I played.

Game Results

The 108,327 fans in Beaver Stadium witnessed Penn State come from 18 points down to shock the Buckeyes and hand Paterno win number 324. And forgive Mills for being humble. He more than played a role. He ran the show.

It was only 13-9 at half, a placekicker's struggle. Ohio State struck first in the second half on Jonathan Wells' 65-yard touchdown jaunt, followed two minutes later by Ross' 45-yard interception return for a score. 27-9 visitors.

State wasted no time responding. On the ensuing series, Mills— he'd entered the game on the second series and played so well that Paterno later said he felt he had to stay with him—optioned right, cut upfield, sprang over a teammate, bounced off a block, and sprinted 69 yards for six points. The two-point conversion failed, but the Lions kept coming, adding a 26-yard Mills-to-Tony Johnson score with less than five minutes to play in the third. The score: 27-22 Buckeyes.

Penn State started its next possession on its own 10-yard line, moving to midfield with help from a 13-yard pass to running back Omar Easy. On the first play of the fourth, Mills hit tight end Luke for 31 yards. On the very next play, Mills to McCoo put Penn State on top for good, 29-27.

Not that the game was over. First Penn State's defense picked off Ohio State quarterback Steve Bellisari. A series later, State forced a punt. When Gould missed a 48-yard field goal with 6:59 remaining, the Bucks responded, driving to Penn State's 34 with 2:55 showing. But Mike Nugent's attempt to steal back the lead for Ohio State never took flight; instead his 51-yard field goal attempt hit the outstretched hands of PSU's Jimmy Kennedy.

After the Lions ran out the clock, bedlam ensued. Paterno had his milestone, and Mills the affection of a delirious crowd. "He leaves me speechless," Tony Johnson said of Mills, who rushed for 138 yards and threw for 280 that day. "Sometimes I just sit back and shake my head at what he does."

For weeks Paterno had downplayed passing Bryant, but in the aftermath, the scene was too special to overlook. "You never think it's going to be a big deal until it happens like this, with this many people," he said after Penn State awarded him a ring bearing "324" and announced plans to construct a statue of the then 74-year-old on the east side of Beaver Stadium's concourse. "I'm a very, very lucky guy to be at an institution such as Penn State."

The win briefly changed the program's momentum—the Lions won three of their final five, foreshadowing a 9-4 year in 2002—and solidified Mills as starting signal-caller. It was a situation he says was smoothed by support from Senneca. "I was very close with Matt, and I couldn't have asked for a better person to be in that situation with," says Mills, whose career took off in 2001 and '02, but was marred by injury, inconsistency, and criticism during much of his final two campaigns. "When he lost his starting job, he could have been an a—hole, but he was the complete opposite. He lived above me, and after the Ohio State game, he came down and he's like, 'Obviously I'm extremely disappointed and I want to be playing. But I don't want this to get between our friendship. If they think you should be playing, it's fine, and I support you 100 percent.'"

Reflecting on State

There are undoubtedly things Mills misses about Penn State and others he does not. That comes with the territory for a guy who played hurt more times than he cares to remember. Mills was pegged as the savior after a dismal 2001 season, then led State back to a bowl and the Top 25 in 2002, only to see it all crumble again in 2003 and '04, when Penn State went a combined 7-16. It's no way for a senior co-captain to go out, but Mills, who heard far more boos than cheers in his final season of college ball, holds no grudges.

"I definitely don't miss [the boos], but it's something that's helped me grow into the person I am today," says Mills, a kinesiology major who went undrafted in 2005, then tweaked a hamstring and was cut early by the Washington Redskins during their rookie minicamp. "Watching Senneca do it helped. I learned a certain way to handle it."

Even so, the rollercoaster of a career and the stress of trying to catch on with an NFL team left him "burned out mentally." He spent much of the fall of 2005 rehabbing—his hamstring and psyche. He moved home to Maryland, took a break, debated quitting football, did some radio work, and even flew to Vegas to play in the World Series of Poker (he lasted deep into the second day).

His future? He hasn't fully given up on a dream of playing pro—even Arena or NFL Europe ball—but in 2006, he put that chance on hold to apply for graduate assistant coaching positions at several college programs, ultimately landing a grad position on the coaching staff at Temple. It's part of his long-term goal to teach and coach, and no, there's no spite in his tone when discussing Penn State or potentially working there someday. (Penn State was one of the schools to which he applied for graduate assistant work.) In fact, ask about the good times, and he quickly relates stories about those magical Northwestern and Ohio State wins, or an electric win against Nebraska in 2002. "Talking about those days gives me chills," he says. "When I turn on the TV or go up for a game, I definitely miss it."

And believe it or not, some Nittany Lion fans miss him, too.

ACKNOWLEDGMENTS

T hank you to James Reeser, sports editor at the Wilkes-Barre *Citizens-Voice*, for his insider's knowledge and careful editing throughout this effort. Thanks as well to author and Penn State historian Lou Prato for his advice and occasional access to his Rolodex.

Thank you to Mike Franzetta with the Football Letterman's Club for helping me track down many of these Nittany Lions past, and to Sandi Segursky and the rest of the staff in the Penn State football office for their kind assistance with my every request. Also thanks to Brian Siegrist with Penn State Sports Information, who consistently went above and beyond to help me pull this project together.

And last, thanks to the players you'll read about in the pages to come who agreed to share with me the pieces of their lives called Penn State football.

CREDITS

Chapter 1, Wally Triplett
> Quote 3, *mhsrodis.com*, history of Midland Borough, PA.
> Quote 9, *Dallas Times Herald*, courtesy *Penn State Football Encyclopedia* by Lou Prato

Chapter 2, Rosey Grier
> Quote 6, *Penn State Alumni News*, Sept. 27, 1954
> Quote 11, *USA Today*, Feb. 1, 1993

Chapter 3, Galen Hall
> Quote 8, *San Antonio Express-News*, Aug. 24, 2003
> Quote 9, *The Birmingham News*, Aug. 27, 2000
> Quote 10, *Pittsburgh Post-Gazette*, Dec. 28, 1999
> Quote 11, *The Philadelphia Inquirer*, courtesy *Penn State Football Encyclopedia*
> Quote 12, *The Birmingham News*, Aug. 27, 2000

Chapter 4, Lenny Moore
> Quote 6, *The Philadelphia Inquirer*, courtesy *Penn State Football Encyclopedia*
> Quote 9, *The Philadelphia Inquirer*, courtesy *Penn State Football Encyclopedia*
> Quote 11, *Pittsburgh Press*, courtesy *Penn State Football Encyclopedia*

Chapter 5, Joe Paterno
> Quote 3, *Sports Illustrated*, Dec. 22, 1986
> Quote 7, *Sports Illustrated*, Dec. 22, 1986
> Quote 15, *No Ordinary Joe* by Michael O'Brien
> Quote 16, *Pittsburgh Post Gazette*, Sept. 11, 1998

Quote 17, *Sports Illustrated*, March 15, 1976
Quote 18, *Centre Daily Times*, Oct. 28, 2001
Quote 22, *Sports Illustrated*, Dec. 22, 1986
Quote 23, *Pittsburgh Post Gazette*, Sept. 11, 1998

Chapter 7, Charlie Pittman
Quote 14, *The Post-Standard* (Syracuse, N.Y.), Feb. 8, 1991
Quote 15, *Austin American-Statesman*, Dec. 25, 1996
Quote 16, *Austin American-Statesman*, Dec. 25, 1996

Chapter 8, Lydell Mitchell
Quote 6, *St. Louis Post-Dispatch*, Dec. 14, 2003

Chapter 9, John Cappelletti
Quote 5, Usstudentathletes.com, Heisman speech excerpt

Chapter 10, Todd Blackledge
Quote 6, *The New York Times*, Nov. 29, 1981
Quote 7, *The New York Times*, Nov. 29, 1981

Chapter 11, Mike Munchak
Quote 17, courtesy *Penn State Football Encyclopedia*
Quote 18, courtesy *Penn State Football Encyclopedia*

Chapter 12, Gregg Garrity
Quote 8, *Sports Illustrated*, Jan. 10, 1983
Quote 9, *Sports Illustrated*, Jan. 10, 1983
Quote 10, *Washington Post*, Jan. 2, 1983
Chapter 13, Shane Conlan
Quote 2, *Buffalo News*, Oct. 26, 2005
Quote 3, *Los Angeles Times*, Sept. 10, 1987
Quote 12, *Orange County Register*, Jan. 1, 1987
Quote 13, *Sports Illustrated*, Jan. 12, 1987
Quote 14, *Sports Illustrated*, Jan. 12, 1987
Quote 15, *St. Petersburg Times*, Nov. 12, 1991
Quote 16, *Sports Illustrated*, Jan. 12, 1987

Quote 17, *Associated Press*, Jan. 4, 1987

Chapter 15, Bucky Greeley
Quote 11, *Sports Illustrated*, Oct. 24, 1994
Quote 12, *Centre Daily Times*, Oct. 9, 2004

Chapter 16, Joe Nastasi
Quote 4, *Chicago Tribune*, Nov. 19, 1995
Quote 5, *Associated Press*, Nov. 19, 1995

Chapter 18, LaVar Arrington
Quote 7, *Sports Illustrated*, Aug. 16, 1999
Quote 8, *Sports Illustrated*, Aug. 16, 1999
Quote 9, *Centre Daily Times*, Jan. 2, 2000
Quote 10, *The Daily Collegian*, Jan. 11, 2000

Chapter 19, Zack Mills
Quote 7, *Philadelphia Daily News*, Nov. 1, 2001
Quote 9, *Pittsburgh Post-Gazette*, Oct. 28, 2001
Quote 10, *Associated Press*, Oct. 28, 2001